LEITH'S BOOK OF DESSERTS

LEITH'S BOOK OF DESSERTS

VALERIA V. SISTI

FOREWORD BY PRUE LEITH

PHOTOGRAPHS BY GRAHAM KIRK

BLOOMSBURY

First published in Great Britain in 1997
Bloomsbury Publishing Plc, 38 Soho Square, London W1V 5DF

A CIP catalogue record for this book is available from the British Library

ISBN 0 7475 3176 5

10 9 8 7 6 5 4 3 2

Photographer: Graham Kirk
Assisted by: Giovanni Campolo
Stylist: Helen Payne
Home Economist: Puff Fairclough
Assisted by: Jacqui Thomas, Eithne Neane, Philippa Munro, Gina Forshaw

Typeset by Hewer Text Composition Services, Edinburgh
Printed in Great Britain by The Bath Press, Bath

CONTENTS

ACKNOWLEDGEMENTS

I consider myself a very lucky person to have had the help of such talented and professional people when writing *Leith's Book of Desserts*.

Caroline Waldegrave made it all possible and I'm forever grateful to her and the staff at Leith's, particularly to Eithne Swan and C.J. Jackson for organizing all the recipe testing and to Celia Francis for her dessert ideas.

I thank Richard Mayson for the excellent wine text and suggestions and also Graham Kirk, Giovanni Campolo, Helen Payne, Jacqui Thomas and Puff Fairclough, for the great photographs.

At Bloomsbury a huge thanks to David Reynolds for the unconditional support he has shown for my ideas, and to Monica Macdonald for her patience and flexibility. Helen Dore kindly guided my words into their proper places and I thank her deeply for it. I'm also honoured by the wonderful foreword Prue Leith wrote for the book.

Heartfelt thanks goes to my family and friends in Brazil, France, America and England for their support and encouragement; in particular to my husband Richard.

Finally, to my mother, Auzônea Rosa Vieira: this book is for you.

FOREWORD

Since I no longer own Leith's School of Food and Wine in London, I feel free to praise its products to the skies. One of those 'products' is Valeria Sisti, who came to us first as a student, later worked as a teacher, and now, while teaching or demonstrating at the school, occasionally writes cookbooks. This is her second. The first was *Leith's Latin American Cooking*, written with passion and purity, which was a great success.

All Leith's books are reliable. Hugely experienced editors, a dozen teachers and a hundred students make very critical testers and tasters. But this book is much more than a collection of fail-proof, delicious recipes. Valeria is fascinated by social history, and the myths and rituals that come with everyday ingredients. Her chapter on Guilt, in which she explains our modern-day neurosis about 'bad-for-you' foods, is masterly, ending with the welcome words, 'Once we know why we behave the way we do, that our fears and phobias are a result of our cultural and social background, the enjoyment of food seems to be within our grasp again, especially of the so-called "bad" foods, like sugar, butter and cream.'

And so say I! What a relief to find a book unashamedly devoted to the most delicious and wonderful puddings and desserts, made as they should be made with real sugar, real butter, good chocolate and proper double cream.

To my mind, the thing that matters more than anything else in cooking is the desire of the cook for excellence. What is the point of a morning's slaving over a hot stove if the result is to be only half-nice because you bowed to current 'correctness' and omitted or replaced the ingredients called for?

Valeria's desserts are little masterpieces. They will give pleasure to diner and cook in equal measure – the real treat of eating perfection, matched by the lasting satisfaction of having produced it.

Prue Leith

CONVERSION TABLES

The tables below are approximate, and do not conform in all respects to the conventional conversions, but we have found them convenient for cooking. Use either metric or imperial measurements. But do not mix the two.

Weight

Imperial	Metric	Imperial	Metric
¼oz	7–8g	½oz	15g
¾oz	20g	1oz	30g
2oz	55g	3oz	85g
4oz (¼lb)	110g	5oz	140g
6oz	170g	7oz	200g
8oz (½lb)	225g	9oz	255g
10oz	285g	11oz	310g
12oz (¾lb)	340g	13oz	370g
14oz	400g	15oz	425g
16oz (1lb)	450g	1¼lb	560g
1½lb	675g	2lb	900g
3lb	1.35kg	4lb	1.8kg
5lb	2.3kg	6lb	2.7kg
7lb	3.2kg	8lb	3.6kg
9lb	4.0kg	10lb	4.5kg

Australian cup measures

	Metric	Imperial
1 cup flour	140g	5oz
1 cup sugar (crystal or caster)	225g	8oz
1 cup brown sugar, firmly packed	170g	6oz
1 cup icing sugar, sifted	170g	6oz
1 cup butter	225g	8oz
1 cup honey, golden syrup, treacle	370g	12oz
1 cup fresh breadcrumbs	55g	2oz
1 cup packaged dry breadcrumbs	140g	5oz
1 cup crushed biscuit crumbs	110g	4oz
1 cup rice, uncooked	200g	7oz
1 cup mixed fruit or individual fruit, such as sultanas	170g	6oz
1 cup nuts, chopped	110g	4oz
1 cup coconut, desiccated	85g	3oz

Approximate American/European conversions

	USA	Metric	Imperial
Flour	1 cup	140g	5oz
Caster and granulated sugar	1 cup	225g	8oz
Caster and granulated sugar	2 level tablespoons	30g	1oz
Brown sugar	1 cup	170g	6oz
Butter/margarine/lard	1 cup	225g	8oz
Sultanas/raisins	1 cup	200g	7oz
Currants	1 cup	140g	5oz
Ground almonds	1 cup	110g	4oz
Golden syrup	1 cup	340g	12oz
Uncooked rice	1 cup	200g	7oz
Grated cheese	1 cup	110g	4oz
Butter	1 stick	110g	4oz

Liquid measures

Imperial	ml	fl oz
1 teaspoon	5	
2 scant tablespoons	28	
4 scant tablespoons	56	
¼ pint (1 gill)	150	5
⅓ pint	190	6.6
½ pint	290	10
¾ pint	425	15
1 pint	570	20
1¾ pints	1000 (1 litre)	35

Australian

250ml	1 cup
20ml	1 tablespoon
5ml	1 teaspoon

Approximate American/European conversions

American	European
1 teaspoon	1 teaspoon/5ml
½fl oz	1 tablespoon/½fl oz/15ml
¼ cup	4 tablespoons/2fl oz/55ml
½ cup plus 2 tablespoons	¼ pint/5fl oz/150ml
1¼ cups	½ pint/10fl oz/290ml
1 pint/16fl oz	1 pint/20fl oz/570ml
2½ pints (5 cups)	1.1 litres/2 pints
10 pints	4.5 litres/8 pints

Useful measurements

Measurement	Metric	Imperial
1 American cup	225ml	8fl oz
1 egg, size 3	56ml	2fl oz
1 egg white	28ml	1fl oz
1 rounded tablespoon flour	30g	1oz
1 rounded tablespoon cornflour	30g	1oz
1 rounded tablespoon caster sugar	30g	1oz
2 rounded tablespoons fresh breadcrumbs	30g	1oz
2 level teaspoons gelatine	8g	¼oz

30g/1oz granular (packet) aspic sets 570ml/1 pint liquid.

15g/½oz powdered gelatine, or 3 leaves, will set 570ml/1 pint liquid. (However, in hot weather, or if the liquid is very acid, like lemon juice, or if the jelly contains solid pieces of fruit and is to be turned out of the dish or mould, 20g/¾oz should be used.)

Wine quantities

Imperial	ml	fl oz
Average wine bottle	750	25
1 glass wine	100	3
1 glass port or sherry	70	2
1 glass liqueur	45	1

Lengths

Imperial	Metric
½in	1cm
1in	2.5cm
2in	5cm
6in	15cm
12in	30cm

Oven temperatures

<table>
<tr><th>°C</th><th>°F</th><th>Gas mark</th><th>AMERICAN</th><th>AUSTRALIAN</th></tr>
<tr><td>70</td><td>150</td><td>¼</td><td rowspan="4">COOL</td><td rowspan="5">VERY SLOW</td></tr>
<tr><td>80</td><td>175</td><td>¼</td></tr>
<tr><td>100</td><td>200</td><td>½</td></tr>
<tr><td>110</td><td>225</td><td>½</td></tr>
<tr><td>130</td><td>250</td><td>1</td><td rowspan="2">VERY SLOW</td></tr>
<tr><td>140</td><td>275</td><td>1</td><td rowspan="2">SLOW</td></tr>
<tr><td>150</td><td>300</td><td>2</td><td>SLOW</td></tr>
<tr><td>170</td><td>325</td><td>3</td><td rowspan="2">MODERATE</td><td rowspan="2">MODERATELY SLOW</td></tr>
<tr><td>180</td><td>350</td><td>4</td></tr>
<tr><td>190</td><td>375</td><td>5</td><td>MODERATELY HOT</td><td rowspan="2">MODERATE</td></tr>
<tr><td>200</td><td>400</td><td>6</td><td>FAIRLY HOT</td></tr>
<tr><td>220</td><td>425</td><td>7</td><td>HOT</td><td rowspan="2">MODERATELY HOT</td></tr>
<tr><td>230</td><td>450</td><td>8</td><td rowspan="2">VERY HOT</td></tr>
<tr><td>240</td><td>475</td><td>8</td><td rowspan="2">HOT</td></tr>
<tr><td>250</td><td>500</td><td>9</td><td rowspan="3">EXTREMELY HOT</td></tr>
<tr><td>270</td><td>525</td><td>9</td><td rowspan="2">VERY HOT</td></tr>
<tr><td>290</td><td>550</td><td>9</td></tr>
</table>

INTRODUCTION

I don't have a sweet tooth yet I enjoy desserts. I'll explain. Desserts to me have the same importance as the main course, if not more. The dessert is the dish that will finish a meal in great style and leave a lasting impression on the guests.

Most people when planning a meal start with the main course or the wine and work a menu around it. I start with the dessert and then decide what would complement it well. If the main course turns out to be rather mediocre, a great dessert will save the evening: if the main course is a success, the dessert will make the evening especially memorable. All the recipes in this book are accompanied by my suggestions for a complementary main course.

There is a good choice of desserts for every occasion. Some can be prepared almost, if not totally, in advance, and are great for buffet parties; they can sit for a while on a buffet table without looking tired and are easy for people to help themselves. Classic choices like chocolate roulade or meringue baskets filled with fruit and cream can be made really special if served with raspberry or white chocolate and orange sauce.

Recipes that need very little or no last-minute assembling include lemon and lime fudge tart with crème fraîche, frozen chocolate mousse cake with fresh berries, praline and chiboust frozen loaf with raspberry sauce, or orange ice cream with pine-nut sablés. New ideas can be served alongside the classic favourites, like caramel pecan tart or cocoa and raspberry flan with whipped cream.

For larger dinner parties a good idea is to offer a selection of two to three different desserts, always including a classic – Normandy apple flan or tiramisù for example – and a more bold option, such as coconut meringues with guava and honey sauce.

The choice is also dictated by fruit in season. Fresh and dried apricot tart, and warm nectarine and fromage frais feuilletées are great summer recipes, while grilled figs with mascarpone ice cream, and apple and walnut pie with Cheddar pastry make wonderful autumn desserts.

Fruit, yoghurt and most bought ice creams are nice, but they are not real desserts. Real desserts excite our eyes, make our mouths water and stay in our memory long after we have eaten them. They are made with the freshest ingredients, seasonal or exotic fruits, and prepared in a way to combine different flavours, textures and even temperatures in perfect harmony.

The best desserts, the ones we tend to remember for a long time, are usually homemade. There is something very special about a homemade dessert, a flavour of real ingredients that cannot be matched by even the very best bought ones. A simple homemade apple crumble with custard or cream will definitely please more than any frozen concoction available in the supermarket, designed to be put in the oven at the last minute.

Desserts are easier to make than most people think, and can invariably be completely or partially prepared in advance. Some of the recipes in this book are very simple, some are intended for more special occasions and are more elaborate. In the notes to the recipes I give suggestions for how far ahead they can be prepared or whether they can be frozen.

My aim has been to offer delicious, exciting, easy-to-make desserts that will stimulate the senses and make a lasting impression by the pleasure they provide. I have not been concerned with cutting down on sugar, butter or cream. There is just enough of these in the recipes to make them taste great – no more but certainly no less. Together with chocolate, they are the most common ingredients used in desserts, and I have therefore included chapters tracing their culinary history and myths, nutritional value and uses in the kitchen. I have also written a chapter on Guilt, explaining how we are in danger of becoming a society that cannot enjoy food for its own sake, and suggesting how preparing and serving desserts can help rectify this.

Desserts are an indulgence, an escape from routine. Most of us don't drink champagne every day, so when we do, we tend to savour it slowly, almost solemnly. The same should apply to real desserts – they are not something we eat every day, but when we do, it should be with reverence.

Human beings can only perceive four tastes – sour, sweet, acid and bitter – and are innately attracted to sweet and repelled by bitter. Taste is also organically linked to our sense of smell and our memory. If you are passing in front of a bakery, for example, the smell of bread being baked will automatically remind you of what fresh bread tastes like and probably of when you last had it. Although recent research shows that we cannot remember a flavour for more than ten years, gustative memory plays an important part in our lives. The sense of taste is one that outlasts most of the others, like hearing, sight and sexual desire. 'Show me another pleasure which comes every day and lasts one hour,' the eighteenth-century French politician Talleyrand said of food in his old age. Remembering that combined sensations of taste and smell will be stored in our gustative data base for the next ten years, we should make an effort to ensure they are special.

In this book you will find classic dessert recipes from traditional favourites, like lemon meringue pie, to relative newcomers like tiramisù. There are seasonal fruit desserts, winter specials and simple light summer desserts. The idea is to offer a repertoire of recipes from pies and tarts to ice creams, sorbets, sauces and biscuits, with suggestions for different combinations. All the recipes are accompanied by wine writer Richard Mayson's wine suggestions, and he has also contributed a comprehensive chapter on dessert wine.

The recipes were a great pleasure to create, write and test. The research involved in the writing of the text also opened many doors to understanding why we eat the way we do, and explaining our phobias and apprehensions. I hope it will serve the same dual purpose for you, offering on the one hand a new set of ideas and recipes for delicious desserts, and on the other, the facts about why we can enjoy them without guilt.

GUILT

This chapter attempts to outline the cultural, social and historical reasons why in the West over the last decade we have developed such mixed feelings towards food and eating. Today guilt seems to be present whenever eating is involved, but it is undoubtedly experienced most strongly when we eat desserts. We might think this is a modern trait, but in fact it was expressed as early as the Book of Revelations: 'It was in my mouth as sweet as honey: as soon as I had eaten it, my belly was bitter.'

Different religions have used food as a moralizing tool for centuries – from its use as sacrifice, a link between man and the gods, to the concept of consubstantiality: becoming what you eat. For example, pork was prohibited to the Jews and Muslims, who considered the pig filthy animal, and the Aztecs ate the hearts of their captured warriors believing that by doing so their force and bravery would be transferred to them.

The religious prohibitions on food became law to millions of people, and to break those laws by eating the forbidden food meant sinning, and by implication culpability. The Catholic Church prohibited a number of foods during Lent, in particular red meats, hence the idea of fish as holy and healthy, since it was the only meat allowed during Lent. Most religions adopted a particularly strong stance against foods that gave pleasure, like sugar and alcohol, some going as far as prohibiting the consumption of honey to their followers because it could ferment in the stomach and become alcoholic.

With the loosening of the Catholic grip on Europe and the advances of science, the last hundred years have seen the birth of the modern believer; someone who can rationalize the reasons for food bans and disregard them without much guilt. The cause/effect of sinning and feeling guilty still applies, but on nutritional, not religious grounds. Moral views on food today have switched from religion to nutrition, but although such views are more specific and backed by science, the moral overtones are the same, if not stronger. Fat, salt and sugar – the reviled trio – are followed closely by convenience and junk food.

Along with religion, cultural and socio-economic differences have been the main factors forming society's phobias and guilt towards such a basic necessity as food. 'What we eat, when we eat it and how we eat it is always defined by the customs and validated by various prohibitions and obligations of a religious nature.'[1]

[1] Apfeldorfer, *Je mange, donc je suis.*

Socio-economic differences change our perception and therefore our views on accepting or rejecting a particular food. Sugar is a very good example of this. In the days when it was occasionally used as a remedy or as a rare spice or seasoning at the tables of the very wealthy, the only people who could afford it, it was considered a healthy, invaluable ingredient. During the seventeenth century when its production and consumption became widespread, and its price fell sufficiently to make it available to all, rumours and myths against its use began to circulate. From that time Europe became divided between the saccharophobes and saccharophiles. The English upper class, the largest consumers of sugar since the fifteenth century, suffered a reverse effect, and developed a strong aversion for it as soon as it became available to the lower classes. Even today, a large sugar intake is considered a lower-class habit. The French, who consumed less sugar than the English (the theory being that wine-producing countries have less appetite for it), were on the whole saccharophiles. This position has changed little – French, Italians and other continental Europeans seem to have a more relaxed approach towards sugar consumption, with the result that they still eat less of it than the English.

Our acceptance of the effects of food on our bodies is also determined by social factors. In the Middle Ages, when food was scarce and its production uncertain, being overweight was seen as a status symbol, a visible sign of belonging to a wealthier class of people who could afford to feed themselves well. This idea is still valid in poor and underdeveloped countries.

In the affluent Western countries, where the availability of food is secured, being overweight means quite the contrary statistically. Research shows that as many as 50 per cent more overweight people belong to the underprivileged classes. In childhood, there is no significant weight difference between the classes. As children grow to puberty, the weight of girls from richer backgrounds goes down drastically, while there will be very little difference in the weight of boys.

The pressures of middle- and upper-class values in food terms are especially evident in relation to women. It is amongst the more well-to-do white families that the highest incidence of eating disorders, in particular anorexia nervosa, manifests. This brings us to the main problems of society versus nutrition today: the role of women and their expectations regarding their physical image.

More than 60 per cent of women now work outside their home. They are also expected to be responsible not only for food preparation, but for buying and planning the family meals. To be able to cope with such tasks, the modern woman has to rely increasingly on ready or convenience foods, which becomes a potential source for a sense of failure, followed by guilt, towards her family and herself.

This sense of failure comes from the

acknowledgement of the widening gap between what women know to be a healthy and adequate diet, with what they actually buy, prepare and put on the plate. This feeling of failure is thoroughly studied and exploited by the food industry. Its aim is to help, so it claims, hence the variety of ready-prepared foods. This very sophisticated industry also capitalizes on guilty feelings by demanding premium prices for ready-prepared salads, vegetables, soups, sauces, and so on; at the same time, although these products have undergone some sort of processing, they are perceived as much better than frozen or canned foods. The fact that they have to be stored in the refrigerator and have a sell-by date, seems to appease our conscience. They are fresh and perishable, therefore they must contain few or no preservatives. They are the closest thing to 'homemade' we can get without making it ourselves. We have transferred the care and time needed to prepare a meal to the careful checking of the sell-by dates on chilled prepared foods in the supermarket in order to secure the freshest ones.

The role of family nutritionist is one that many women take very seriously. Eating as a family is considered by many as the last binding element in today's society. When cooking becomes more and more difficult due to lack of time, to cook a proper meal from scratch is seen as a display of love towards the family – if they reject your food, it is your love they are rejecting. That is sometimes the reason why family meals can develop into nervous and stressful occasions.

Women are surrounded by food all the time, from planning, buying and finally preparing it. So when it is also demanded of them to stay slim by dieting or not eating the same food they prepare for the family, no wonder so many eating disorders and guilty feelings begin to appear. We are all caught in the dilemma of eating, enjoying food and becoming slightly overweight and rejected by society, or rejecting food and the bonding with family and friends it provides, while keeping slim and accepted by all. Food becomes dissociated from pleasure, and from health as well.

Freudians believe food and sex are very closely linked. The first pleasurable sensation we experience is the sucking of our mother's milk. Food and sex are associated in many ways – most substances considered aphrodisiacs are foods, and sex rituals can involve food – naming sexual parts with foodstuff names, for example. Sex and pleasure seem to be more closely linked with sweet foods, a taste for which is also perceived as a feminine trait (men usually offer chocolate or sweets to a woman, rarely the other way around). Societies that disregard sex, usually also disregard food: 'Victorians considered food, like sex, an unfortunate carnal necessity to be endured. Neither activity was to be enjoyed, but simply performed.'[2] Victorian society was also

[2] MacClancy, *Consuming Culture*.

very pious and adhered rigidly to high moralistic values.

Morality and sex remained in opposition until the early 1950s and the invention of the Pill. Until then, the all too obvious consequences of free sex, especially for women, was a way of keeping them in line within the moral standards established by society. The Pill brought sex with no consequences, sex and pleasure were finally permissible, and during the sixties and seventies sex gradually became guilt-free (at any rate until the Aids era) and lost most of its moralistic overtones. But these were transferred to food, and nutrition as a science was born with the objective of advocating health through eating. Just as pregnancy was evidence of sinning in a moralistic society before the Pill, today obesity is a public and unavoidable display of transgression against the rules of good and healthy eating. As a matter of interest, anorexia nervosa was first recognized as a disease in the late nineteenth century, while bulimia, an eating disorder which does not have perceptible symptoms, was not diagnosed until as late as 1980. 'Eating disorders, such as anorexia nervosa, bulimia, compulsive eating and laxative addiction, make up a sorry list of the female condition in the industrialized west of the late twentieth century.'[3]

The United States was, and still is, the generator of most of the good/bad food ideas, and with very good reason. In America the statistics of death caused by cancer, heart disease and overweight-related illnesses are alarming – in 1992 over 64 per cent of Americans were considered overweight. Food was declared the number one public enemy and treated accordingly.

For the past thirty years the world press has been disseminating information about the goodness or badness of almost all the foodstuffs found on our planet. While half the American laboratories are busy trying to incriminate some foods, the other half are trying to prove the contrary. Food means big business, and to counteract the harmful effects of adverse publicity, producers have formed unions and boards (meat, dairy, sugar, etc.) and also finance and publish scientific reports on the nutritional qualities of their own products. As a result, we have been bombarded with conflicting information on nutrition, and not surprisingly, most people do not know what or whom to believe.

Examples abound: in the 1970s white bread was considered bad, fattening and making no real contribution to a healthy diet. Fibre was 'in': a change to high-fibre breads was the order of the day. Ten years later, white bread is back: there are now reservations about too much fibre in the diet, and white bread has a high calcium content in any case. And so the list goes on: fats, oils, a wide range of fruits and vegetables, not to mention all the cancer-inducing effects of food preservatives and colourings.

The late 1970s and the 1980s became

[3] Ibid.

the decades of food scares and phobias. Although as previously mentioned the saccharophobe has existed since the nineteenth century, the lypophobe (someone who fears fat) is a very modern creature. The cholesterol scare began in a coronary-blocked America, again in an attempt to make Americans aware of the dangers of overeating. In the 'land of plenty', research showed that as many as 6 per cent of the population were highly deficient in fundamental nutrients, both in the higher- and lower-income classes.

Nutrition is a young and developing science. There is, however, already a consensus based on a few rules for a healthier way of eating. Unfortunately, the information made available to the public is dictated not only by their right to know, but also by commercial interests.

For many people, food that tastes really good means it is not healthy. The Anglo-Saxon countries seem to have adopted a stronger moral tone on food consumption. The obese are still seen as people who cannot control their food intake, although there is enough scientific evidence to show that a variety of other factors can contribute to a person becoming overweight.

Some theories suggest that foods like sweets and chocolates are regarded in a bad light by moralistic societies simply because they provide a source of pleasure that is cheap, easily available and, being solitary and intense, of a highly individual nature. Such an image is reinforced strongly by advertising for chocolate – Cadbury's Flake, for example, in which the outside world does not count when the woman is eating the Flake, and we can witness her immense pleasure. This is invested with sexual overtones – to feel pleasure with strong sexual connotations alone is seen as a sin, and sinning involves guilt. The French go so far as to call a chocolate binge a *petit péché* (small sin). People tend to think that anything that brings such enjoyment has to be bad for you. Sinning against the Church has been replaced by sinning against oneself, by breaking all those nutritional 'laws' of healthy eating we are made so much aware of nowadays.

The 1980s saw the birth of the propagators of the healthy creed: the 'health evangelists'.[4] These crusaders of the good health gospel are avid readers of all the literature available on nutrition, they know all the chemical formulas of the dreaded saturated fats, all the E numbers and what they mean – they are true believers in the 'Tell me what you eat and I'll tell you who you are' dictum. For them sugar is poison, fat is death, and so on. We have all met someone like this at least once, at a dinner party when you are happily attacking your chocolate mousse. You can feel those incriminating eyes and that healthy look and that the person is bursting to tell you all about the dangers of chocolate eggs, cream, sugar and all the other foods you have so much enjoyed during the meal.

[4] Tannahill, *Food in History*.

The difficulty of following the rules set by the nutritionists is that for the majority of people this will mean an almost complete destruction of a way of life and all its complex social relations. The great majority of English people, for example, still eat too many eggs, sausages and chips. The French still eat, drink and probably smoke as heartily as ever. The Americans are growing fatter each year. That does not mean to say that nothing has changed: indeed it would be difficult to find a person in Western society who is not aware of the dangers of cholesterol, of consuming too much processed food, and so on. What seems to be slowly changing are attitudes towards received information. The 'commandments' of healthy eating are known to almost all, but a great number of people choose to ignore them.

The food scares have stopped scaring simply because they are no longer taken as a sure and lasting fact. The myth or image that equates beauty with slimness has been tainted by the horrors of the physical and psychological consequences of eating disorders like bulimia and anorexia nervosa.

From the beginning of the 1990s a change in the way we see and consume food seems to have slowly been taking place. The main focus now is balance. In food terms, this means that we can eat everything, but in moderation. Gone are the diets based on just one type of food (grapefruit, brown rice, pineapple, etc.). Even red meat and wine can now be safely consumed, but in moderation.

Until recently, sophisticated restaurants were seen as providers of unhealthy food with a strong emphasis on butter and rich sauces. This view has changed drastically in recent years. More and more cooks, food writers, celebrity chefs, restaurants and food magazines are passing on their concern for more healthy eating in the form of alternative ingredients, health-conscious recipes and information.

Moderation and variety seem to be key words in today's view of healthy eating. To be deprived of a particular food that we like increases our wish to have it, not only 'bad' foods like sweets or chocolate, but simple and healthy food such as potatoes and bread. Temptation is particularly hard to resist in view of how readily available food is in Western society. So we try to replace it by eating the low-on-everything alternatives. Most people feel dissatisfied after eating low-fat, low-sugar desserts, and the tendency is to eat more of them, which ultimately makes us ingest as many calories as if we had eaten the real thing from the beginning. So welcome real desserts, but in moderation!

Eating may seem a mechanical habit: feed the body with the right amount and type of food and it will work perfectly. Well, it isn't quite that simple. Our appetite, the feeling of satiety and intensity of pleasure – or the opposite – when eating a certain type of food is regulated by a gland situated at the base of our brain, called the hypothalamus. So food and pleasure are organically and intrinsically linked, whether we like or not.

Another organic function beyond our control, but fundamental to the way we eat and of particular interest in the context of this book, is also performed by the hypothalamus gland. When we have had enough food, the hypothalamus sends the signal to the brain informing that our stomach is full (this takes from fifteen to twenty minutes, so eat slowly and you will probably eat less), at which stage we think we could not eat anything else. However, when faced with the desserts trolley or menu, for example, a new type of appetite appears. Although we still could not eat another spoonful of stew, for example, we can happily tuck into the ice cream. The variety of food stimulates the hypothalamus which then creates a hunger sensation for this new food. That is one of the reasons why Westerners eat too much, they are overstimulated by the enormous choice of foods provided by the food industry.

Being faced with so much choice also creates an inverse behaviour pattern: again, a good example is ice cream. With dozens of different flavours to choose from, it is incredible that vanilla still commands more than 40 per cent of ice-cream sales. Confronted with so much choice, many consumers tend to go back to what they already know and like.

The aim of this book is to do the same: to go back to enjoying what we know and like. Desserts that taste like desserts, ice creams that taste like fresh cream, pies that taste of fruits or nuts and real butter, not low-fat and sugar substitutes of unknown origin. Once we know why we behave the way we do, that our fears and phobias are a result of our cultural and social background, the enjoyment of food seems to be within our grasp again, especially of the so-called 'bad' foods like sugar, butter and cream.

BUTTER

The word butter comes from the Greek *bou-tyron*, meaning 'cow-cheese'. Sheep and goats were domesticated about 10,000 years ago by farmers in Mesopotamia, and cattle around 2000 years later. Although butter can be made from the milk of most mammals (with the exception of the camel), cow's milk is the most commonly used in the West. In Africa and Asia, the milk of buffaloes, goats, ewes, mares and even donkeys is used to make butters that in general have a stronger flavour than cow's-milk butter.

THE HISTORY OF BUTTER

Known since antiquity, butter was introduced to Greece by the Scythians, who were cattle herdsmen. However, the Greeks, who were avid consumers of olive oil, considered butter to be a barbarian food and used it only as a remedy for healing wounds. They also preferred milk and cheese made from goat's and sheep's milk. The Indians used butter to cure wounded elephants in the first century. In Europe, it was used as an ointment to soften skin, to grease hair and keep lice away. Melted butter left outdoors for a few days to go rancid was drunk as a remedy for arthritis.

Throughout the centuries butter has acquired symbolic connotations in different cultures. In ancient Egypt it was rare and expensive. Everything that was oily and shiny was considered a symbol of wealth, so a lump of fatty incense or perfumed butter was placed on the head and allowed to melt and drizzle voluptuously down the face and body. In India, butter is the precious product of the sacred cow and as such treated with reverence and used in many rituals. For Buddhists, clarified butter symbolizes the ultimate development of the spirit of Buddha.

The people of Europe have been divided for centuries into northerners (butter-eating and cider- and beer-drinking) and southerners (oil-eating and wine-drinking). This clear-cut division still persists today to some extent, and is due to biological and cultural factors.

Most humans are born provided with an enzyme called lactase, which has the function of digesting milk sugar, called lactose. Once old enough to eat other foods, two-thirds of the world's population becomes lactose-intolerant, which means that they cannot digest milk in its raw state. In this way nature assures the survival of the species, with the milk being left for the newborn. People from China, Japan, the Americas and Oceania are for the most part lactose-intolerant, a fact that is reflected in their cuisine, where very little milk is used.

Through the generations the other third of the world's population, mostly people from the northern hemisphere, the original cattle herders from thousands of years ago who relied heavily on milk and dairy produce for their food, became lactose-tolerant and passed the trait to their offspring. To put it in a simplified way, our bodies need vitamin D to maintain strong bones and teeth and absorb calcium from our diet. This presents no problem to people living in areas where there is a lot of sunshine, since the sun helps the body to absorb vitamin D through the skin, but people who live in the cold and sunless northern areas do have a problem. Lactose helps the absorption of calcium, so people from the north became tolerant to milk not only from lack of other foodstuffs, but because they needed to in order to keep healthy bones and teeth.

Although dairy products like cheese, yoghurt and soured cream are all low in lactose and can therefore be consumed by people with lactose intolerance, they are also usually avoided. Greeks, Jews, Arabs and some Mediterranean people have a cultural aversion to cow's milk, not a biological one.

From the time of the Greeks and Romans until the Middle Ages little record remains of the uses made of cream or butter. The earliest cookery books in the fourteenth century show an almost total absence of these, not only in France and England, but also Italy and Spain. Although it is known that some local production of butter became widespread throughout Europe, it was eaten mainly by peasants and until the fifteenth century was rarely used in the most affluent households. There is evidence that during days of plenty most people preferred lard or suet, and in poverty oil was favoured.

Taillevant, the famous fourteenth-century chef to Charles V and author of the book *Le viandier*, used butter in only just over 1 per cent of his sauce recipes. Most medieval sauces contained no butter or cream. They were of a very acid nature, using large quantities of vinegar, spices and verjuice (an acid sauce made from the juice of unripe grape mixed with lemon juice and spices). During the fifteenth century, butter gradually featured more widely in Italian and French cookery books, but it was only during the next two centuries that its use became firmly established in France and England. In England, until the Industrial Revolution, there were plentiful supplies of butter in the cities, but like oysters, it was consumed mainly by the poor. One result of this was a deficiency of vitamin A in the more affluent classes, who suffered commonly from bladder and kidney stones.

With the Industrial Revolution and the shift of land labour to the city, butter became more and more expensive and slowly took over the tables of the wealthy, a fact that can be seen in the cookery books of the seventeenth century. Although acid sauces were still widely eaten, butter ones began to appear and quickly multiply, especially to accompany fish dishes. Butter was used in 80 per cent of the sauces in a cookbook dated 1674.

The Catholic Church banned butter during Lent, which created a big problem for the people who lived in the north. The 'butter chest' was created, allowing the wealthy a dispensation of the ban in exchange for a monetary donation to the Church. A magnificent example of how northerners preferred to pay rather than give up eating butter is the Butter Tower of Rouen Cathedral in northern France. The option for those who could not pay was to change to oil, to the delight of the merchants of southern countries who, according to some sources, profited from an easy outlet for poor-quality oil unsold in the south.

During the Middle Ages and the Renaissance butter-making could be a fraudulent business. Being a highly perishable commodity and with no refrigeration available, butter was made locally in rural areas and consumed daily. To provide the large cities with butter, many tricks were employed. In order to mask the rancid taste of old or badly made butter, it was washed down with milk and water and salted again. There was no hygiene control and adulterations abounded. For example, lard, water and large quantities of salt were added to make it keep longer when transported: a source dating from 1305 reveals that one pound of salt was added to every 10 pounds of butter, which meant that it was common practice to wash the butter thoroughly with water before it was edible. Colourings were also added to make butter look fresh: a favourite was a paste made with marigold flowers and salt which was added to winter butter. Other colourings were carrot juice, saffron and annatto.

Butter was sold at market stored in earthenware pots covered with salt water, or wrapped in sorrel or herb leaves. It was prohibited to sell it on a fish stall. In some cities, a cow was brought to the house door where it was milked and the butter made on the spot.

The Dutch, Danes, Irish and English were among the largest consumers of butter in Europe. The Dutch (who were called 'buttermouths' by the English) were, and still are, the largest producers of butter in Europe. Together with the English, the Dutch were the first settlers in North America, taking with them their fondness for eating butter. It was not uncommon for these early Americans to take a cow with them when they travelled in order to have supplies of fresh butter.

Northern Europe became associated with power and wealth, with cultural and economical domination by England, the Netherlands and Germany for long periods, and since all these peoples were dairy produce-eaters, by extension their cuisine was considered to be more refined, while the food from the south, with its abundant use of olive oil, had the connotation of being rustic and peasant-like. The people from the south, however, believed for many centuries that eating butter caused leprosy, so it is no wonder that they avoided it, to such an extent that people would take supplies of oil with them when they had to travel north.

The last decade of the nineteenth century saw a great step forward towards making butter of even quality constantly available. This was achieved by isolating the lactic acid bacteria and using it in a controlled way, assuring a consistency in quality. (Until then, the cream, once separated from the milk, was left to 'ripen', taking up the bacteria from the air.) By 1908 the Danes were already producing most of their butter by this method and the rest of the dairy farms in Europe soon followed suit.

HOW IS BUTTER MADE?

Butter is made by shaking the milk cream or the milk itself until the fat globules come together, in the process called churning. Churning was probably discovered by accident when herdsmen carrying milk in animal-skin containers found their milk transformed into butter after a bumpy journey. Before industrialization, making good-quality butter required special skill, judgement and strength.

The butter churn invented in the early Middle Ages was still in use during the nineteenth century. It consisted of a narrow, upright wooden tub with a lid, through the centre of which ran a long wooden rod fitted with a perforated attachment at the bottom. The person doing the churning would stand over the tub and pound the plunger up and down in the cream with regular and precise speed until the cream was turned into butter, when it was said that the butter had 'come'. This had to be done at the right temperature, 12–18°C/53–64°F. Since there was no way of controlling the temperature, churning time varied according to the seasons – when the weather was stormy or hot it could take hours.

All the work involving dairy produce was done by women: the word dairy derives from the word *dey*, which means a female servant. While all the work in the fields was a men's job, milking, cheese-making and churning were regarded as indoor work, therefore allotted to the women. Some women were considered to have a special gift for butter-making, known as having 'cool hands'. They were usually very strong and skilled in their churning – a very good asset for marriage in rural areas.

Apart from the skill of making the butter, the breed of a cow and its feed greatly affected the final taste. The different types of pasture changed not only the taste but also the colour of the butter. Cows that ate lots of buttercups, for example, produced a butter with a particular yellow tinge. Generally, winter butter was very pale, and summer butter quite yellow.

Milk for making butter was left to

stand while the cream rose to the top and it was then scooped out. The best butter was made from cream that had been scooped out first, and inferior-quality butter from a second scooping, called 'after-butter'. The cream was then left to mature or 'ripen', which could take from three to seven days. The ripening increased the lactic flavour, making a stronger-tasting butter than the type we eat today, which is usually made from 'sweet' (unripe) cream with added lactic acid.

Once the cream was ripe enough (after no less than three days), it was made into butter. During churning the cream separated into butter and a liquid called buttermilk, which could be heated and its remaining solid content strained off to make hard cheese. In wealthy households, buttermilk was used to feed the pigs: pigs fed in this way were considered to give the best-tasting meat.

When the churning was finished, the butter was kneaded to expel any buttermilk still enclosed in the fat (buttermilk has a high proportion of casein or curd and was a major cause of rancidity) and then washed until the water ran clear. The butter was salted by soaking it in a brine solution and then draining it well, or by working dry salt into the butter.

Ideally, butter should never be touched with the hands while it is made, so a large number of wooden implements were devised, such as the butter scoop and paddles of boxwood, called Scotch hands, to lift, mould and press the butter into pots for home use or to shape it for sale. Each region had its own particular way of shaping, from cylinders that were cut into portions, to conical or egg shapes.

BUTTER IN THE KITCHEN

Most butter today is made from pasteurized cream with added milk lactic acid. The cream does not 'ripen' as it did before industrialization, and the result is a butter with a very milky flavour compared to the type our ancestors used to eat.

Butter is sold unsalted or salted. Salted butter will keep longer, but both freeze well for up to nine months. Salt and refrigeration will slow down the process of rancidity, but will not stop it completely. There are two types of rancidity: one caused by the butter absorbing the smell and flavours of other food (hydrolytic) and the other by the chemical reaction that takes place when butter is in contact with air (oxidative). Butter absorbs flavours and smells of other foods very easily, a characteristic used to advantage with garlic butter, and herb and sweet butters for use in cooking. However, butter that has become rancid by oxidation is biologically unacceptable to humans and can be the cause of serious health problems.

The use of butter in cooking is extensive and very important. In cake-making, for example, butter is fundamental to improve keeping qualities, to add flavour and give a soft texture. Butter is also used to enrich sauces and to prevent food from sticking to pans.

Butter burns at a lower temperature (121°C/250°F) than most oils, due to the residues of milk protein it contains. To increase its cooking temperature, add some oil to the cooking pan or clarify the butter by removing the milk solids (see below).

Even refrigerated butter will turn rancid: to delay this process, butter should be kept in a covered container avoiding contact with air, or wrapped in foil to avoid absorbing the smells from the other foods in the refrigerator. Unsalted butter is usually a little more expensive than salted because it keeps for less time, but it can be used in any recipe, while salted butter should be avoided in more delicate recipes where the salt will interfere with the final flavour (hollandaise sauce, buttercreams and fine biscuits, for example).

Butter contains a minimum 80 per cent fat, of which two-thirds is saturated. Weight for weight, butter contains nearly twice as many calories as proteins and carbohydrates. Although a good source of vitamins A and D, it should be used sparingly (a minimum of 30g/1oz a day) to cut down on calories and control cholesterol in the diet.

In its combination of flavour, texture and smell, there is no substitute for butter. At least 400 volatile compounds make up the butter aroma, which means it is almost impossible to achieve a chemical equivalent.

Margarine was invented by a Frenchman in 1869 as a cheaper alternative to butter. By law today, margarine has the same proportion of fat and water (80 and 20 per cent) as butter. It was originally made of beef fat and skimmed milk, but the recipe has evolved greatly since then. Today most margarines are made of a mixture of vegetable, fish and animal oils or pure vegetable oil (usually an oil high in polyunsaturated fats, such as sunflower or soy). The aim of the margarine industry has always been to make it taste, smell and look like butter, which is an almost impossible task. However, some brands of margarine make a good substitute for people trying to cut down on their cholesterol intake and it can also be used successfully in baking, roasting and almost all types of cooking, except deep-frying. The criticism of margarine has always been that we don't really know what its components are. These include added flavourings, emulsifiers, vitamins, salt and colourings which keep it from going rancid and make it spreadable even when cold.

In this book, butter is the only fat used, not only because it tastes better than margarine, but also because butter has fewer food additives. There is no intention of advocating the use of large quantities of butter with a corresponding increase in cholesterol or calorie intake: although there is no denying that butter is used widely in the recipes, they are meant for the occasional treat, not to be eaten daily. I strongly believe that only real butter or cream can provide the right flavour and achieve the same level of satisfaction in eating desserts. If concern with calories and cholesterol is too important to be forgotten even occasionally, my advice is: eat less, but eat the real thing.

TYPES OF BUTTER

Unsalted or sweet butter: butter made without the addition of salt. It will keep in the refrigerator for up to a week before it starts to turn rancid, and it can be frozen successfully for up to 9 months. Imported French butter is called *doux* (sweet).

Salted butter: sweet butter with added salt. It will keep a little longer than sweet butter if stored properly. It also freezes well for up to 9 months.

Clarified butter: butter that has been separated from milk particles and other impurities which cause it to look cloudy when melted, and to burn easily when heated. It keeps for up to 3 months if refrigerated and it can be used in recipes where butter needs to reach high temperatures. It can also be used as a seal on pâtés or potted meats. To clarify butter: put 250g/9oz butter into a saucepan with a cupful of water and heat until melted and frothy. Pour into a bowl and allow to cool and set solid, then lift the butter, now clarified, off the top of the liquid beneath. Another method is to heat the butter until foaming without allowing it to burn. Pour it through clean fine muslin or a double layer of 'J' cloth.

Ghee: almost the same as clarified butter, but flavourings such as dried chillies, seeds and spices can be added. The melted butter with its added flavourings is left over a very low heat for up to 45 minutes or until the milk sediments have become slightly browned, which gives the ghee a nutty flavour. The liquid is then carefully strained and can be kept at room temperature for weeks. Ghee is the basic fat used in Indian cooking.

CREAM

WHAT IS CREAM?

Cream is produced from whole milk and has all the nutrients of milk – protein, calcium, carbohydrates and fat – but in different proportions. As milk fat is lighter than water, it rises to the surface and can then be skimmed off, which is how cream can be made at home: allow whole milk to stand for about 24 hours and the fat will rise to the surface. Although easy enough for home use, this method leaves still a large quantity of fat in the milk. Commercially, cream is separated from the milk mechanically through a process of centrifuging: the cream, which is heavier than the milk, gravitates towards the centre, separating from the milk; both are released through two different outlets. A controlling valve will determine how much fat has to be removed from the milk.

The minimum fat content for each variety of cream is controlled by law, with the percentages varying from country to country. While single cream has around 72 per cent of water for 21.1 per cent of fat, double cream has around 48 per cent of each fat and water. Cream is labelled according to its percentage of fat.

Like milk, the basis of all dairy produce, cream undergoes a series of processes to secure its safety for human consumption. The most common are the following:

Pasteurization: a process which kills the bacteria present in milk. The milk is heated to 72°C/160°F, kept at this temperature for 15 seconds, then cooled down immediately and quickly to below 5°C/40°F. Apart from killing any harmful bacteria, pasteurization improves the keeping qualities of milk. It has very little effect on flavour and nutritional value and is applied to all types of fresh milk before being bottled or cartoned.

Homogenization: a process that breaks down and distributes the fat globules evenly throughout milk or cream (it is not needed when the cream is of a high fat content). It prevents cream from separating during storage but homogenized cream does not whip well, since the fat is already broken up and will not hold any air. Homogenization produces a smoother, creamier and more easily digested milk or cream. Homogenization takes place before pasteurization.

UHT (ultra-heat treatment) or Long Life: homogenized milk or cream that is subjected to an ultra-high temperature of 132°C/266°F for 2 seconds or more, which destroys all the bacteria, making it sterile, and then rapidly cooled and vacuum-packed.

Sterilizing: milk or cream that are first

homogenized, canned, and then heated to 72°C/162°F for 60 minutes before being cooled. All micro-organisms are killed. The final product has a 'cooked' flavour and a creamier colour than fresh milk or cream. It is the process that will make milk or cream keep longer.

DIFFERENT TYPES OF CREAM

DOUBLE CREAMS

There are three types of double cream, all with a minimum of 48 per cent fat content and pasteurized.

Double cream: the content is not homogenized and the cream will keep, sealed, in the refrigerator for 2–3 days (summer) and 3–4 days (winter). It has a thick but pouring consistency, and it can be whipped more easily if a small amount of milk is added first (1 tablespoon milk to 150ml/¼ pint cream).

Thick double cream: this is heavily homogenized cream, quite thick in texture, which has the same fat content as double cream. It does not pour easily and does not whip. It will keep as for double cream above.

Extended life double cream: this is homogenized cream, vacuum-sealed in bottles. Keeps for 2–3 weeks in the refrigerator. It can be whipped.

WHIPPING CREAM

Halfway between single and double cream, it has a fat content of around 35 per cent and is not homogenized. It is only used for whipping and it whips to twice its volume.

SINGLE CREAM

With a minimum of 18 per cent fat, single cream is homogenized and does not whip. It should not be boiled or it will separate. Used as a pouring cream to enrich sauces, accompany fruits and cereals, or in coffee.

STERILIZED CREAM

With a fat content varying from 12 per cent (half-cream) to 23 per cent (sterilized cream), this is made with homogenized cream. It keeps for up to 2 years unopened, but once opened should be treated as fresh cream. The half-cream type has a pouring consistency with a slight caramel flavour from the processing, while the sterilized type is thicker and usually spooned. It does not whip.

LONG-LIFE CREAM

Also with varying fat content, 18 per cent (single cream), to 35 per cent (whipping cream). Both types are homogenized and packed in foil-lined containers. They are the closest to fresh cream in flavour and texture. Unopened, long-life cream keeps for up to 8 weeks. Once opened, treat as fresh cream. To whip long-life whipping cream, chill the cream, bowl and whisk well. It takes longer to whip than fresh cream.

SOURED CREAM

Cream that has been artificially soured with the addition of a culture bacteria to give a particular sour taste. It has the texture of thick cream but has a fat content of 18 per cent, so it should not be boiled or it will separate. Keeps for up to 7 days in the refrigerator.

CLOTTED CREAM

A speciality of the West Country, clotted cream has the highest fat content of all creams, around 55 per cent. It has a distinct yellow colour and is quite thick. It is made by heating milk in shallow pans over boiling water for about 1 hour and allowing the milk to cool slowly. The fat crust formed on the surface of the milk is scooped out and is known as clotted cream.

HALF CREAM

With a fat content of 12 per cent, this is homogenized and sold as 'coffee cream' or 'top of the milk'.

WHIPPED CREAM

With a fat content of 35 per cent, this type of cream is usually sold frozen and contains added sugar.

AEROSOL CREAM

Homogenized UHT cream that is packed in aerosol containers, with nitrous oxide used as a propellant gas to 'whip' the cream. It increases to four times its volume and should be served immediately because it loses its bulk very quickly. It keeps in the refrigerator for up to 3 months.

IMITATION CREAM

Usually made from emulsified vegetable fat, with added dried egg, gelatine and flavourings. It looks like cream and is widely used in the catering industry.

WHY DOES CREAM WHIP?

The fat in cream is made up of small globules suspended in the milk. Each of these globules is surrounded by a thin membrane of protein and fat that is filled with tiny air bubbles when the cream is whipped. The cream becomes stiff when some liquid fat is released from the globules, causing all the air bubbles to stick together. When cream is over-whipped, the fat globules release too much liquid, making the air bubbles collapse and forming large clumps. There is no way of correcting over-whipped cream.

If the cream is too thick, it will become over-whipped before there is enough time to pump the air bubbles into the fat globules. Double cream can be diluted with a little milk (see above) to make its fat content lower. Whipping cream (see above) has an average fat content of between 35 and 40 per cent, whipping to twice its volume. To get a good result the cream should be fresh and cold. Once whipped, cream can be kept in the refrigerator for a day or piped into shapes and frozen.

SUGAR

Native to Polynesia, sugar cane was known in China, India and Greece as far back as 2500 BC. It was also known to the Romans, who only consumed it in its plant form: small pieces of sugar cane were peeled and then chewed and believed to be an aphrodisiac. It was in India, around 700 BC, that cane was first refined into sugar. From India it was taken by the Persians to countries like Syria, Egypt, North Africa, Sicily and southern Spain, where its production was quickly established. It was not until the eleventh century that sugar cane was introduced to Europe from the Arab world by the Crusaders, reaching England in 1319.

Up to the end of the fifteenth century sugar was a costly luxury item, used mainly to make medieval medicines palatable. Together with salt, it was used as a spice or seasoning at the tables of the very wealthy. Both salt and sugar had a very restricted culinary use; usually just a little was sprinkled over a dish after it had been cooked. There was no real distinction between sweet and savoury courses as the dishes were all placed on the table at the same time and diners would grab whatever they could from the dishes in front of them.

Through the Crusades and the spice trade which used routes in the Arab world, a love for very sweet things slowly began to manifest. The Arabs introduced sugar, citrus fruits, almonds, saffron and rice to Spain. Almond-based recipes like marzipan, nougat and *torrone* are direct imports from Arab cuisine, and sugar gradually began to be used as an ingredient rather than just as a seasoning. But it would take almost 300 years, an emigration of an estimated 9 million Africans as slaves to the New World, and the almost complete extermination of the native Indian population of the Caribbean islands before sugar became readily available on the world's table.

Massive sugar production and consumption have been surrounded by controversy from the beginning. When sugar cane was introduced by Columbus to the new continent in 1493, little could be foreseen of the far-reaching consequences of the Africanization of the Americas. Sugar cane is a huge grass, almost like a bamboo, with succulent stems which are the source of the cane sugar. It is an essentially tropical plant that grows best in damp, warm climates, hence its production in places like Cuba, Jamaica, Dominican Republic and Hawaii. The plant has erect stems 2–4 metres/6–12 feet or more in height, and the process of extracting the syrup, boiling and preparing it for refining was more than any native Caribbean Indian or European settlers were able or willing to do.

The link of the great maritime nations of the time, Portugal and Spain, with Africa was already strong and the Portuguese were using slaves (although not all Africans) in their sugar plantations in Madeira, Azores and São Tomé, so the idea of transporting enslaved Africans to work in the sugar, cotton, tobacco and coffee plantations soon became a reality. The Africans, used to the hot climate, were considered strong and docile workers and they quickly became a very important economic asset to the colonies.

For centuries honey had been the most used form of sweetening in the majority of the European and Mediterranean countries. Egyptian tomb reliefs of the 3rd millennium BC already showed the collection of honey by smoking the bees from their nests, but bee husbandry as such did not start until around 650 BC. Mead or honey-ale was a widespread drink throughout the Middle Ages, especially in countries that did not then produce wine, such as England and Germany.

Bees were kept in most monasteries for their wax, the only substance accepted by the Catholic Church in candle-making. Honey was an important by-product, especially in England. With the dissolution of the monasteries during the Reformation, the production of honey was greatly diminished in the sixteenth century. At the same time sugar was steadily becoming more available and more popular than other types of sweetener such as syrups and pastes made of figs, grapes and dates. Sugar cane had two great advantages over honey – its preserving qualities and ability to sweeten without flavouring. Honey has a particularly strong flavour, that is imparted to food and especially drinks, and at that time was also full of impurities.

The popularization of sugar came hand in hand with three other new products – coffee, tea, and chocolate (see page 47). All three drinks became very popular mainly because previously non-alcoholic drinks had been mainly restricted to milk and water, the latter being unsafe to drink unless boiled. The new drinks, considered quite bitter, needed sweetening. The production of cocoa, coffee and sugar in the New World increased enormously to supply an ever-growing market. It is estimated that in 1700 Great Britain consumed 10 tons of sugar. A hundred years later the amount increased to 150 tons, mainly because of the increased consumption of coffee, tea and chocolate.

At the beginning of the seventeenth century, sugar was available but still quite expensive. In the next century, as demand as well as production grew, prices fell sufficiently to make sugar a staple product throughout Europe and North America. Its uses were wide-ranging. It was used for medicinal purposes – in healing pastes, for making eye drops, as a laxative, as an ailment for stomach problems, for colds and coughs. Its preserving qualities, for fruit and other types of food, became essential to the kitchen.

HOW IS SUGAR MADE?

The process of making sugar is a laborious one, and was especially so before mechanization.

1. First the canes are harvested and the juice extracted by pressing them between rollers (manual process) or by crushing on a mill (mechanical).

2. The juice (a very thin and watery liquid) needs to be reduced and purified by boiling, during which it will lose 70 per cent of its bulk. The result is a sticky mass of syrup and dark brown crystals.

3. The syrup is then spun at high speed to separate the crystals. The residual syrup is called molasses and is used to make rum. The brown crystals, called raw brown sugar, are then ready to be refined into the different types of sugar now found in the shops (see below).

Whereas today most of the processing is done by machines, 300 years ago it was the labour of the African slaves. The inhuman work conditions – up to 18 hours a day – were considered normal at the time. Bad treatment, exhaustion and malnutrition were the way of life for the sugar plantation slaves in the Americas. The sugar trade became synonymous with slavery, and the moral issue of consuming sugar, given the appalling conditions of its production, began to create heated moral discussions, especially in England.

Even before the continental blockade and the Napoleonic wars, the French and Germans were looking for a substitute for sugar cane. In 1747 the German A. Margraft discovered the existence of common sugar in many root vegetables, of which the type *Beta vulgaris*, beet sugar, had the most concentrated amount. The advantage of the beet sugar is that it grows in a temperate climate, which meant sugar production was no longer exclusive to the tropical colonies in the New World. It was not until 1830–40 that the sugar beet industry became well established in France but it then spread quickly to the whole of Europe. Sugar beet looks like a turnip and the first step in processing it into sugar is washing and shredding the roots. They are then soaked in hot water, which draws all the sugar out of the plant. This sugary water is then boiled and the water evaporated, leaving behind a concentrated sugar syrup, also called molasses. The final process before refining is spinning, to separate the sugar crystals from the molasses, resulting in sugar with identical structure, taste and appearance to those of cane sugar.

SUGAR AND NUTRITION

How has an ingredient so well thought of for centuries become one of the most reviled in modern Western society? How have we become so obsessed with the idea that sugar is so bad for us?

From the twelfth week of gestation, a foetus can already distinguish sweetness, a taste inbred in humans. From the first taste of his mother's milk, a baby develops a desire for sweetened drinks. Nutritionists will argue that there is enough 'natural' sugar in almost all foods for there to be no need to add refined sugar. But sociologists and anthropologists will reply that as a specifically human characteristic, the learned love for specific food items can override biologically predetermined preferences: culture overcomes nature. And that is where most of the problems regarding the consumption of refined sugar lies.

Eating behaviour and its related diseases have become a vast area of research involving nutritionists, psychologists, sociologists and doctors who are trying to understand the consequences of global addiction and/ or phobias to foods like sugar and fat by looking at racial and geographical differences. The uniformization of ideas, ideals and images through the vehicles of commercial culture like television and cinema also play an important role in our eating habits.

Westerners eat an average of 1kg/2lb refined sugar per week, of which as much as three-quarters comes from manufactured foods. Modern civilized society relies more and more on these convenience foods. Cooks will agree that it is difficult to make large quantities of food taste and look good. So food manufacturers use considerable amounts of flavourings, chemical ingredients and sugar to enhance flavour and improve the appearance of food. Sugar is included in the composition of some unlikely-sounding foods, from sausages to pasta sauces, not to mention all the foods like breads, cereals, fruit juices, etc. where one can actually taste the sugar and could well do without it.

Whenever we eat something, the level of blood glucose (sugar) in our body is raised, and is then released slowly and steadily during digestion, keeping the whole body system in balance. When we eat refined sugar (i.e. quick sugars, including alcohol), it is absorbed very quickly, raising the blood glucose to very high levels. The pancreas then sends insulin into the bloodstream to normalize or lower the blood-sugar level, causing a rapid fall in the latter which leaves a craving for more sugar.

When the blood sugar is at a high level there is a general feeling of energy that is quickly followed by fatigue, mood-swing changes and, in more severe cases, even fainting. The constant sugar-craving vicious circle is a very dangerous one. When fed only with high-sugar, low-fibre foods the body will gradually stop producing the enzymes necessary to digest fibre proteins and carbohydrates, thus creating a dependency on the high-sugar, low-fibre foods which the stomach can easily digest, and resulting in an unbalanced and unvaried diet: most manufactured foods high in fat and sugar are low in fibre. However, a person would need to eat up to 2kg/4lb of refined sugar a week for an extended period of time before the digestive system is adversely affected, which leads one to conclude that addiction to sugar is chemical rather than psychological, although the psychological effects are the most apparent.

All the above considerations are based on the ingestion of sugar in the form of snacks eaten between meals or as 'pick-me-ups'. When a normal amount of alcohol or a dessert is consumed with or after a balanced meal, the effect is different, mainly because all the other major nutrients, including fibre, proteins and carbohydrates, will be there to secure normal blood-sugar levels, and the symptoms of 'quick sugar' intake are avoided.

In fact the human body does not need refined sugar in order to survive; it can take all it needs from other sources like fruits and vegetables. The aim should be to decrease the amount of the refined sugar we add to our food, as well as the intake of manufactured foods that are full of 'hidden' sugars. By doing so, we can sensibly control our intake of refined sugar and minimize its effects on our bodies.

Although refined sugar contains no nutrients, it is not harmful in itself. In 1986, the US Food and Drug Administration categorically stated 'there is no evidence at all to link sugar with obesity, diabetes, high blood pressure, hypoactivity or heart problems'; the only danger of eating sugar is the possibility of tooth decay. Shakespeare already knew that: 'Sweet, sweet, sweet poison for the age's tooth,' said King John.

Nutritionists have agreed on what constitutes the principles of a good diet, but there is still a lot of conflicting information, creating a large number of sceptics who discard all the information passed on to them through the media and assume a lifestyle based on the principle of enjoying all foods, even though there is a risk that some will cause health problems in the long run.

Desserts and sweets have become a tool of reward and punishment, which gives 'real foods' like vegetables, meat and fruits the characteristic of being good for you but not necessarily appetizing, thus perpetuating the fetish for sweet things. This applies particularly to children, who use the consumption of sweets as a form of rebellion against the established nutritional rules imposed on them by adults.

Our perceptions of pleasure and eating are linked from day one. A taste for sweet things has often been thought of as a feminine characteristic. Brillat-Savarin, the French gourmet, wrote in 1825: 'There is not a woman, especially if she be well-to-do, who does not spend more for her sugar than for her bread.' In fact both boys and girls like sweets, but as they grow to adulthood, girls usually turn to cakes, pastries and chocolate, while boys turn to alcohol. As we know, the result on the body is the same: bursts of energy and a general feeling of well-being, however short-lived.

There is no secret formula for how to enjoy all types of food and stay slim; the answer seems to be moderation. Many people regard sugar as the culprit in a variety of problems such as obesity, hyperactivity, dependency on drugs, to name just a few. This modern fixation on trying to find one substance to be charged with all the problems caused by the way we eat and live, shows not only ignorance of the latest scientific research, but also lack of an overall view of how the body can be affected by other things apart from food, like stress, pollution, loneliness – we are what we eat, but how and where we eat also contribute significantly to our overall physical and mental fitness. Yet sugar seems to be the first ingredient to go when the diets begin; we have stubbornly elected it as the cause of those unwanted extra pounds, forgetting the importance of more significant and lasting changes to our way of eating and living as the way to a healthier and sane body. The long-term harm done by constant dieting is surprisingly more damaging than a few extra pounds on the scale. People who are happy with their weight, even if they are slightly over the medical chart weight/height limit, and who eat a varied and balanced diet, statistically have a higher chance of living longer than people who are forever unhappy about their weight and follow restrictive and unbalanced diets.

A new approach is beginning to emerge within the medical world. Research shows that the constant-dieting behaviour pattern makes us dislike food because it comes to represent an obstacle between ourselves and the idealized body we so much desire. Even when we succeed in shedding those pounds, the fact that we need to keep eating to stay alive, makes us dissociate pleasure from food; food becomes a constant threat of becoming fat again, however careful we are in what we eat. This has a long-term effect on our character, making us more narcissistic and rigid in our manners and attitudes towards the outside world. We cannot dissociate pleasure from eating without producing long-term psychological effects on our personality, so the sensible approach seems to be to develop an awareness of the effects of food on the body, but still to enjoy all the different types of food in a balanced and controlled way.

Food, and sugar, in particular, is not the only cause of the many health problems modern civilized societies are faced with; the sooner we understand all the complex effects on our bodies of how and what we eat, the quicker we will be able to enjoy food as a source of nourishment for the body and of great pleasure for the soul.

SUGAR IN THE KITCHEN

The use of sugar in the home kitchen is mainly as a sweetener, but is very varied. Baking, confectionery and preserving – pastries, cakes and syrups – are some of the areas where sugar is indispensable. Among its many properties are the following:

- It improves the colour of baked goods (cakes, breads, baked hams, etc.), giving them a nice golden colour.
- It prevents the gluten present in flour from developing, making for a softer final product (as in cakes and pastries).
- It preserves (jams, jellies, conserves) by inhibiting the growth of micro-organisms.
- It improves the quality of frozen products, in particular fruit, by preventing the formation of large water crystals.
- It provides food for yeast in breads and yeast doughs.
- It is fundamental in meringue-making because it strengthens the protein in the egg white, helping the mixture to retain a high proportion of air.

Sugar is highly soluble and many of its uses in the kitchen is in the form of syrups. These simple solutions of sugar and water have various strengths according to the ratio of sugar to water. The most commonly used are:

Light syrup: used mainly for poaching and bottling fruit (570ml/1 pint water + 285g/10oz sugar are the classic proportions, but the sugar can be reduced to 110g/4oz for a less sweet syrup).

Medium syrup: for sorbets, ice creams and mousses, and usually made with equal quantities of sugar and water.

Heavy syrup: used in confectionery, e.g. fondants.

As the temperature of the water and sugar increases, an increasing amount of sugar will dissolve. When no more sugar will dissolve at a particular temperature, the solution is said to be *saturated*. As a saturated solution cools, it becomes *supersaturated*. This means that there is a greater concentration of sugar than can easily be held by the water. This may cause the sugar to crystallize.

When the sugar and water solution starts to boil, the water evaporates, making the solution more concentrated in sugar, which has a boiling point higher than water on its own. That is why it is very important to monitor the sugar temperature while making jams, caramels or any sweets, as once the correct temperature is reached the applications of the sugar syrup are very specific. If the proportions are not kept and the water allowed to evaporate, the sugar solution will finish as a caramel or finally as charcoal.

Crystallization only occurs in *supersaturated* solutions, and also if the solution is disturbed. It can be prevented by not stirring the mixture or by adding a small amount of glucose or acid (lemon juice, cream of tartar or vinegar) to the sugar solution before starting a caramel. If small crystals start to form on the sides of the pan, they should be cleaned off with a wet pastry brush, or they will trigger crystallization in the sugar solution.

The addition of butter or chocolate

also slows down crystallization. In some confectionery-making such as fudge the final mixture is beaten as it cools, encouraging the formation of very small crystals, which gives a smooth texture.

It is essential to have a sugar thermometer when making recipes which require a precise concentration of sugar, like fudge or butterscotch. The thermometer should be put into the solution at the beginning of cooking and the temperature checked regularly at short intervals.

Sugar decorations and garnishes add a nice touch to desserts, cakes or pastries. They vary in degree of difficulty from sugar-blowing, done only by professionals, to simply dusting icing sugar over a cake.

SUGAR SYRUP

285g/10oz granulated sugar
570ml/1 pint water
thinly pared zest of 1 lemon

1. Put the sugar, water and lemon zest into a saucepan and heat slowly until the sugar has completely dissolved.
2. Bring to the boil and cook to the required consistency (see below). Allow to cool.
3. Strain. Keep covered in a cool place until needed.

NOTE: Sugar syrup will keep unrefrigerated for about 5 days, and for several weeks if kept chilled.

STAGES IN SUGAR SYRUP CONCENTRATION

TYPE OF SUGAR SYRUP	BOILING POINT	USES
Vaseline	107°C/220–221°F	Syrup and sorbets
Short thread	108°C/225–226°F	Syrup and mousse-based ice creams
Long thread	110°C/230–235°F	Syrup
Soft ball	115°C/235–240°F	Fondant, fudge
Firm ball	120°C/248–250°F	Italian meringue
Hard ball	124°C/255–265°F	Marshmallows
Soft crack	138°C/270–290°F	Soft toffee
Hard crack	155°C/300–310°F	Hard toffee and some nougat
	160°C/318°F	Nougat
Spun sugar	152°C/305–308°F	Spun sugar

NOTE: When boiling to the short thread stage, test by dipping your thumb and forefinger first into cold water. Then dip your finger into a teaspoon of the hot syrup, which should form a sticky thread (about 2.5cm/1in long for short thread) between your thumb and forefinger when they are drawn apart. It is essential that the fingers should be wet when doing this test, to avoid burning them.

TYPES OF SUGAR

WHITE OR REFINED SUGARS

The sugar with the highest purity level (99.8/99.9 per cent). The refining process also removes any trace of nutrients that, though insignificant, are still found in raw brown sugar. The white, odourless and clean-flavoured white sugar comes in a number of different types:

Granulated sugar: medium-sized white shiny crystals with a coarse texture. Larger granules than caster sugar. The cheapest and most common of the refined sugars.
Uses: general purpose (cooking and table). Used for flavouring sugars (vanilla, cinnamon, chocolate) and to make caramel.

Caster (superfine, fine) sugar: fine white crystals made from crushed and sieved granulated sugar. It dissolves more easily than granulated.
Uses: baking, confectionary, pastry, meringues, cakes. The most-used type of sugar in baking and general dessert-making. Also the best for sweetening dairy products, drinks, fruits, etc.

Icing sugar: powdered granulated sugar with the addition of cornstarch or tricalcium phosphate to prevent it from caking.
Uses: meringues, cakes, biscuits, confectionery, icing and decoration.

Preserving sugar: large crystals, specially designed for preserving. The crystals dissolve more slowly and it makes less scum.
Uses: domestic preserve-making.

Jam sugar: Caster or granulated sugar to which natural pectin and/or citric acid has been added to accelerate the setting point of home-made jams.
Uses: domestic jam-making, especially recommended for jams or jellies made with low-pectin fruit such as apricots, plums, strawberries, etc.

NATURAL BROWN SUGARS

Unrefined sugar still containing molasses and with a purity level of 85–99.5 per cent. The impurity is in fact molasses, which gives natural brown sugars their colour and distinctive flavour. They are very important in baking, especially fruit cakes, because they add moistness to the finished product. Although some essential vitamins and minerals are still present in natural brown sugars, they represent a very negligible amount and do not make them nutritionally better than white refined sugars, as is believed by a large number of people.

Demerara sugar: first produced in the Demerara county in Guyana, hence its name. Distinctive large, clear crystals,

sticky due to the molasses content. Aromatic flavour.
Uses: baked goods (apples, crumbles), sprinkled on biscuits and cakes before baking. Also delicious for flavouring yoghurts, fromage frais and porridge.

Muscovado sugar: there are two types:
Dark: sticky fine crystals with a dark brown colour. It has a distinctive strong flavour and should be used sparingly.
Uses: gingerbread, cakes, chutneys, fruit cakes.
Light: same fine crystals as dark muscovado, but a pale creamy colour, due to lower molasses content. Also has a milder flavour.
Uses: ginger biscuits, flapjacks and cakes.

Molasses or Barbados sugar: with a considerably higher percentage of molasses than the dark muscovado sugar, it has a strong flavour and is very sticky.
Uses: as dark muscovado.

SWEET SYRUPS

These are liquid forms of sugar from different sources – sugar cane, corn, maple, etc. They are widely used in the brewing and food manufacture industries.

Corn syrup: derived from sweetcorn kernels. Two types, light and dark, the dark having a more pronounced flavour. A good-for-everything sweetener.
Uses: in a variety of manufactured goods like canned fruits, ice creams, baby foods, preserves, etc. Also in baking, barbecue sauces and jellies.

Molasses: the natural dark viscous syrup with a strong flavour made from the sap of the sugar cane. Less sweet than honey, there are two main types: light and dark (also called blackstrap).
Uses: mainly in baking and toffee-making.

Treacle: a blend of molasses and refined syrup. It is lighter and thinner than molasses but still has a very strong flavour. Ranges from light gold to black.
Uses: in making candies and ginger cakes, and lozenges for the pharmaceutical industry.

Golden syrup: processed liquid sugar with a gold colour and smooth, clear texture. No particular flavour but slightly sweeter than sugar.
Uses: in baked apples and steamed puddings, flapjacks, brandy snaps, biscuit manufacture and brewing.

Maple syrup: made from boiling the sap of the maple tree to a golden colour. Thin, runny and clear, but with a delicious distinct flavour due to a volatile oil it contains. There is no chemical equivalent. The cheaper versions are usually corn syrup that has been flavoured with a small quantity of real maple syrup.
Uses: as a table syrup with pancakes, waffles, ice creams as well as with

baked ham, sweet potatoes or in baking.

REFINED BROWN SUGARS

White refined sugar with added colour and flavour, either from caramel or molasses.

London demerara: larger crystals than granulated sugar, coloured with molasses.
Uses: as demerara.

Soft dark brown sugar: caster sugar tossed in dark-grade molasses or sometimes caramel to give colour and flavour lost during the refining process.
Uses: as dark muscovado.

Soft light brown sugar: milder flavour and paler colour than soft dark brown sugar, treated with lighter-coloured molasses.
Uses: as light muscovado.

CHOCOLATE

Chocolate, derived from the Aztec word *chocolatl* – *choco* (cacao) and *latl* (water) – was the name given to a drink made with cocoa, chillies, water and vanilla, much appreciated by the Emperor Montezuma and his court at the time of their discovery by the Spanish in 1492.

The cocoa bean, from which chocolate is made, is native to tropical America, and recent archaeological evidence indicates that its origins lay in the Gulf of Mexico. The seeds were probably taken to Central America and as far as the Amazon basin where it grows wild. Belonging to the genus *Theobrama cacao* (meaning food of the gods), all twelve species of cocoa are native to tropical America and can only grow in equatorial climates. The common cacao tree is about 8 metres/25 feet high with large, smooth, oblong leaves, tapering at the end. The tree has a particular characteristic: the leaves and clusters of flowers grow straight from the main trunk as well as from the branches, which gives the cocoa pod the appearance of being artificially attached to the tree.

According to Aztec legend, the cacao tree was considered the most beautiful in paradise and its fruit was invested with magical powers to cure disease, quench thirst, nourish and give universal knowledge. From each cluster of flowers usually only one fruit matures. The ripe fruit or pod is ovoid in form, measuring around 25cm/10in long, 10cm/4in wide, and weighing 450g/1lb. Inside a leathery rind there are five cells, and within each cell five to twelve seeds, which are covered in a pink acid pulp. The slimy mass of seeds is extracted and piled in heaps inside baskets or barrels lined with banana leaves or earth, or placed in specially built houses for fermentation. The fermentation will take from one to twelve days, according to the type of cacao bean, and the objective is to destroy the acid pulp, known as mucilage, enveloping the beans. It will also diminish the bitter flavour of te beans, change their colour and start drawing out the first hints of chocolate aroma. When a particularly bitter or strong-flavoured chocolate is desired, the fermenting process is omitted.

Once fermented, the beans are washed and dried. This drying can be done naturally in the sun or artificially. At this stage a process called claying, which consists of coating the beans with a fine layer of clay or earth and then polishing them, improves the appearance of the beans and also helps to remove mildew and any dry mucilage left on the beans after drying. The beans are then ready to be bagged and shipped. The sorting, cleaning, roasting and blending are usually done by the importers to suit the tastes and preferences of their particular markets. Very little has changed in the production and commercialization of cocoa for centuries, and the entire process is not very different from that of coffee production.

THE HISTORY OF CHOCOLATE

Cocoa beans were very important in the economy of pre-conquest Mexico and were even used as a form of currency – a precise number of beans were tied in a bag and the bag used as a monetary unit. Later, in the sixteenth century, the cacao bean continued to be used in this way: 'In the 1540s the charge made for their services by Nicaragua's ladies of pleasure was ten cacao beans'.[1]

From the time of the discovery of the Americas in the 1490s, Spain and Portugal kept a monopoly on the production and consumption of chocolate for over 100 years. The first cargo of cocoa beans to reach Spain from Mexico was in 1524. Slowly its consumption spread to the rest of Europe, and by 1600 cocoa was being exported from Spain to Italy and Flanders.

Chocolate drinking was introduced into Europe at the same time as coffee and tea. In England, the first chocolate house was opened in Oxford in 1650, followed by one in London in 1657. In France, Anne of Austria, wife of Louis XIII, herself very fond of chocolate, tried to introduce it to the French court as early as 1615, but its use only became fashionable during the Regency, under Louis XV, when the French court and high society succumbed to the delights of drinking chocolate and it became a very fashionable drink. 'The Regent's chocolate', a gathering of the aristocracy by invitation from the Regent Philippe of Orleans, was regarded as a mark of great social and political prestige for the chosen few.

The importance of the new drinks was significant in times when foods that were 'heavy in carbohydrates and fats, as most north European foods were, had to be washed down with plenty of liquids, and this was one of the reasons why the Poles, Germans, Dutch and English all acquired a reputation for heavy drinking'.[2] The new 'tropical' drinks provided a welcome non-alcoholic alternative to cider, beer or mead, mainly among the upper classes to begin with and then gradually in the population as a whole. With the appearance of coffee and chocolate houses, a new and very sober era of socializing began. The new drinks were particularly welcomed by upper-class women, and that is one of the reasons why coffee, tea and chocolate houses were usually very luxurious places where they could socialize with other women, or with men in a fashionable and socially accepted way.

[1] Tannahill, *Food in History*.

[2] Ibid.

The most famous of these houses was the Café Procope in Paris. Founded in 1686 by an Italian, it was situated across the street from the theatre of the Comédie Française and with its exquisite and luxurious interior, it soon became the gathering place for intellectuals, artists, actors, politicians and Paris society. Café Procope served a variety of novelty products like coffee, tea, chocolate and ice creams, together with elaborate cakes, pastries and confectionery. In England, cafés were regarded with suspicion to begin with, seen as a way to divert men away from alcohol, but they soon became popular meeting places, and mainly for men.

It was in England that chocolate was first prepared with milk. Sometimes even an egg and Madeira wine were added to it. Until then, water was used as the binding liquid, and the other ingredients varied from country to country.

The Spanish were particularly fond of chocolate and for centuries remained its largest consumer. It was in Spain that the chocolate pot or chocolatière was invented. It consisted of a pot made of silver, porcelain or earthenware, with a conical shape and wooden handle. It had a small spout and the lid was pierced in order to introduce a beater used to create the foam. Chocolatières slowly went into disuse with the creation of eating chocolate and the invention of soluble cocoa powder at the beginning of the nineteenth century, but they can still be found in antique shops throughout Europe.

The method of preparing chocolate as a drink varied greatly. The French added vanilla and lots of sugar; the Italians roasted the cacao bean to a point of bitterness unpalatable to others, much as they do today with their coffee. The Spanish mixed the chocolate with so many other ingredients – some quite unusual ones like chillies – that their recipes were almost impossible to follow.

One Spanish recipe for hot chocolate dating from 1631 includes chillies, cinnamon, rose petals and other flowers, almonds, hazelnuts, sugar and yellow colouring, all finely ground to a paste and then mixed with water to the consistency of a drink. Even though this recipe may sound unusual today, apparently the results were quite delicious, nourishing and not very different from the original Aztec recipe.

It seems that Catholic monks and nuns were also very partial to chocolate drinking, as mentioned in many books and documents of that period. Many of the surviving recipes, which were considered the best or most authentic ones, had their origins in a convent or monastery. There are two reasons for this: first, the Jesuit priests who helped colonize and catholicize the native Indians became very fond of chocolate and were the first to adapt the native Aztec recipe to European taste and bring it back to their mother houses in Europe. Second, the Catholic Church pronounced in 1662 that chocolate drinking was allowed during Lent, provided it did not contain eggs or milk.

From then on, especially in Spain, pious society ladies used to have hot chocolate served to them in church (usually very cold) during the service (usually very long). However, the stimulating effects of chocolate on the Latin temperament were the reason why some Catholic orders, mainly monasteries, also prohibited their members from drinking the 'libidinous brew'.[3]

Because of their novelty or rarity, many of the exotic tropical foods like sugar, tea, coffee, potatoes, tomatoes and chocolate were soon surrounded by myth. Chocolate was believed to be an aphrodisiac, a cure for a number of illnesses, a tonic, a digestive but also, for some, 'a coarse food, only good for the indigenous stomach'.[4] An example of the complete ignorance of the real properties of drinking chocolate can be found in France. As we have seen, members of high society and the aristocracy became avid chocolate drinkers, and when a well-known aristocratic lady gave birth to a dark-skinned baby, who was blamed for the occurrence? The chocolate! We can well imagine that the Belgians (who consume an average 7.2kg/16lb of chocolate a year per head) would constitute a totally different race if such propositions held any truth.

Cocoa beans were sold by weight, and the roasting and blending were done either by the cocoa merchant or at home. After roasting over a fire, the beans were pounded to a paste with water and the other ingredients. The different types of cacao bean were sold separately, and knowledge of the characteristics of each type was very important. Alexandre Dumas, the great nineteenth-century French writer and celebrated gourmet, advised in his vast *Grand Dictionnaire de Cuisine*, published in 1872, that: 'equal parts of Caraque, Sainte-Madeleine and Berbrice cacao beans will make an unctuous, prime quality cup of chocolate'. With the age of mass-produced chocolate we have lost not only the need to know about the different cocoa beans, but also the ability to appreciate their differences (see below).

In the most northern countries like Germany, England and the Netherlands, tea was more popular than chocolate and remained so in relation to coffee as well until very recently. By 1801 'the English each consumed 2½ pounds of tea and 17 pounds of sugar (much of it with tea) a year per head'.[5] The largest chocolate consumers were Spain, France and Austria. Chocolate, like tea and coffee, contains what is now called 'accepted stimulating drugs',[6] and that is another reason for its immense success from the time of its introduction into Europe. Stimulating substances like caffeine were isolated chemically in the nineteenth century, but the general effect chocolate had on the body was

[3] MacClancy, *Consuming Culture*.

[4] *Le Mangeur*.

[5] Hobhouse, *Seeds of Change*.

[6] Ibid.

well documented and appreciated.

In 1825, Brillat-Savarin wrote in his famous work *The Physiology of Taste*: 'It has been shown as proof positive that carefully prepared chocolate is as healthful a food as it is pleasant; that it is nourishing and easily digested; that it does not cause harmful effects to feminine beauty which are blamed on coffee . . . that it is above all helpful to people who must do a great deal of mental work, and especially travellers.'[7] Tea, coffee and chocolate all started as upper-class luxuries, but in a relatively short time became middle-class necessities.

Cocoa was produced in many parts of equatorial America, in particular Central America, Ecuador, Venezuela, Cuba and Brazil. The best cocoa was, and still is, considered to be produced in Venezuela, with the Caracas bean the best. Its cultivation was later introduced on a large scale to West African countries, India and Indonesia. The African continent is today the world's largest producer of cocoa.

Belgium was responsible for the administration of cocoa-producing colonies in Africa in the early 1900s, and created a strong link between the Belgian chocolate industry and the African cocoa bean type. The Belgians are considered to be among the finest chocolate makers in the world, which helped to form the European preference for a stronger-flavoured and slightly bitter chocolate.

Chocolate began to be produced in solid form around the beginning of the nineteenth century, having previously been consumed only as a drink. Around 1820, some of today's well-known chocolate companies were founded, among them Van Houten, Menier, Cadbury, Suchard, Nestlé and Lindt. They were mostly family-run businesses and some remain so today.

With the production of 'eating' or dessert chocolate and its rapid rise in popularity, drinking chocolate was slowly abandoned in favour of coffee and tea. The use of chocolate changed. It became a valuable ingredient in the kitchen for making cakes, biscuits and pastries, and as a flavouring for a variety of recipes.

TYPES OF COCOA BEAN

There are many types of cocoa bean, of which the three most commonly grown are:

CRIOLLO: with a thin skin, pointed pods and plump, pale-coloured beans. The most delicate in flavour and also the most expensive. A criollo can be red (colorado) or yellow (amarillo). The main producers are Central and South America (in particular Venezuela).

FORASTERO: with a thick, harder skin and beans coloured from pale to deep purple. It has a stronger flavour than the criollo and is of an intermediate quality. It has many varieties: cundeamor, liso, amelonado – all with different characteristics in shape. flavour, and yield. The main producers are Brazil and some African countries.

[7] Brillat-Savarin, *The Physiology of Taste.*

CABACILLO: although a variety of the forastero type, the cabacillo is cultivated so extensively that it is considered a variety in its own right – it has smooth, small pods and deep-coloured beans; it gives a large yield and is the cheapest of the cocoa beans, therefore used mainly in the manufacture of candies, cheap chocolates, etc.

The best cocoa is made from the criollo bean. It has a fine and mild flavour and is very aromatic, with little bitterness. Brazilian cocoa, called Maranhao, together with the cocoas from Ecuador and the West Indies, have some bitterness, but they are very useful for making up a good blend with weaker-flavoured cocoas. Most of the African cocoa is from the forastero bean, which has a much higher yield and is considered of inferior quality when it comes to flavour, aroma and other more gastronomic considerations. African cocoa has a particularly bitter and very assertive flavour, preferred by Europeans, while South American cacao with its delicate and gentle flavour is preferred by the North American market.

WHAT IS CHOCOLATE?

Cocoa is a good source of protein, high in carbohydrates, B vitamins and minerals like iron, potassium, copper and calcium. Cocoa butter, the fat found in the cocoa beans, contains no cholesterol, but is high in saturated fats. Chocolate is a high energy food: 110g/4oz dark chocolate contains 470 calories, and the same quantity of milk chocolate 529 calories, and of cocoa powder, 312 calories.

Once sugar, different types of fat and other ingredients like nuts or alcohol are added in the manufacturing process, the nutritional value of cocoa is diminished considerably. The most nutritious way to serve chocolate is as a drink with milk, the proteins in milk complementing those in cocoa.

Dark chocolate contains some stimulating substances, notably caffeine, theobromine, theophylline and also phenylethylamine. They all have complex names but their effect on the body is simple: mildly stimulating and anti-depressant. The amount of caffeine found in a cup of filter coffee varies from 110mg to 150mg. One cup of hot cocoa, made with 1 tablespoon cocoa powder, has about 18mg of caffeine. Chocolate can hardly be blamed for sleepless nights!

The other substances, though, have a more important role, especially phenylethylamine, since it resembles very closely an amphetamine, a well-known component of anti-depressant drugs. Research has shown that addiction to dark chocolate can be a 'natural' way of auto-medication by people of a depressive nature. It is a discreet, very palatable and cheap form of self-medication, at an unconscious level. The doses of those chemicals found in chocolate are minimal and the side effects once the 'medication' is stopped are almost non-existent.

Dried and Fresh Apricot Tart

Chocolate and Almond Tart; Lemon and Raspberry Curd Tart;
Pecan and Sweet Potato Pie

Cocoa and Rasberry Flan

Dried Fig and Pear Filo Tartlets

Puff Pastry Nests with Orange and Caramel Sauce

Warm Nectarine and Fromage Frais Feuilletés

Chocolate Profiteroles

Baked Apple with Maple and Vanilla Sauce

This may seem a simplified way of looking at chocolate addiction, especially when there are so many other social factors that can trigger such eating behaviour – stress, grief, loneliness, to name just a few. It is also important to consider that chocolate addiction usually forms part of an addiction to sweets and sugar in general, with different effects on the body (see page 38). The term 'chocoholic' is often used to describe a person who has a constant or daily craving for chocolate. Research done by injecting phenylethylamine into animals shows a marked tendency towards auto-administration, which could be expressed in human terms as a strong feeling of wanting more and more chocolate and inability to stop eating it once one has started.

HOW IS CHOCOLATE MADE?

Once the cocoa beans have been fermented, washed and dried, the long process of making the chocolate begins. The entire cocoa bean is eaten in some form or other, hence the importance of fermenting, washing, drying and roasting of the different types of bean. The quality of the final product will depend on the care taken during the different stages of preparing the beans and also on the quality of the ingredients added during the manufacture of the chocolate.

The first step is to roast the beans, to develop the flavours and expose the inner section of the bean, called the nib. After roasting, blending different types of bean is done to achieve a particular flavour.

The crushing of the beans comes next. The result is known as cocoa mass or paste, with a fat (cocoa butter) content ranging from 45 to 60 per cent. This paste varies in smoothness and is the raw material for the chocolate industry. The cocoa mass is then mixed with extra cocoa butter, sugar and flavourings and is passed through a series of rollers for blending, the final product being called cocoa solids. At this point the cocoa solids undergo a process called 'conching', invented by Rodolph Lindt in 1879. It involves passing the cocoa mass back and forth through heavy curved rollers at a variable speed and temperature. The rollers used to be shell-shaped (*concha* in Spanish; hence the name). The process can take from a few hours and up to 7 days; the longer the conching the finer, more unctuous and expensive the chocolate will be. Conching is a costly technique that improves the smooth texture and mellow flavour of the chocolate, making what is sometimes known as fondant chocolate. Cheaper brands of ordinary chocolate are generally not conched, having their texture improved by the cheaper means of adding soy lecithin or vegetable fat.

CHOCOLATE PRODUCTS AND TYPES OF CHOCOLATE

From the cocoa mass the following products are made:

Cocoa butter: the natural fat contained in the cocoa bean, extracted from the cocoa mass by crushing it through rollers. It has a pale yellow colour, medium-hard texture and a distinctive chocolate smell. Cocoa butter is the main ingredient of white chocolate and is also added to dark chocolates to improve their texture and enrich the flavour. Pure cocoa butter is also used in the pharmaceutical industry.

Cocoa powder: once the cocoa butter has been extracted from the cocoa mass or paste, a residue, called flakes or cakes, is left. These cakes are grated, making a powder that contains between 8 and 20 per cent cocoa butter, very little compared to other types of chocolate. This process of extracting the cocoa powder was invented by C. J. Van Houten in 1882, and the Van Houten cocoa powder is still considered one of the best. Cocoa powder is usually sold unsweetened and is used widely in baking as an enhancer of chocolate flavour and colour. If stored in a tightly sealed container, it will keep for up to a year.

Plain chocolate: made of a mixture of cocoa paste, butter and sugar, it contains a minimum 43 per cent cocoa solids, which can rise to as much as 70 per cent in some very good brands. It is sold as bittersweet or bitter chocolate, according to the amount of sugar added. It is aged for at least 6 months after it is made in order to develop its full flavour. Wrapped tightly and stored on a cool place, it will keep for up to a year.

Milk chocolate: plain chocolate with full-cream milk powder added. It has a lower percentage of cocoa solids (around 35 per cent), so it is best for eating rather than cooking where its flavour will be diluted. It is aged for only a month after it is made, and if properly stored will keep fresh for up to 6 months.

Baking chocolate: also called cooking or unsweetened chocolate. It is basically solid cocoa blocks or slabs. There is no addition of sugar or any other ingredient and it is produced for the chocolate manufacturers who will then add their own choice of extra ingredients.

Couverture chocolate: meaning 'covering' in French, this chocolate is made with a top-quality sweetened cocoa paste and has a smooth texture with a high proportion of cocoa butter. It is used by professional confectioners as a coating chocolate, but it needs to go through the tempering process (see page 57) before being used, in order to retain its shiny and glossy appearance. It is available plain, milk and white.

White chocolate: made with cocoa butter, sugar and full-cream milk powder, this is technically speaking not a chocolate since it contains no cocoa mass, hence its colour. White chocolate is difficult to work with, but it makes very nice contrasting decoration for chocolate cakes and dark chocolate recipes.

Drinking chocolate: sweetened cocoa powder, sometimes with added milk powder and different flavourings. Not to be used interchangeably with cocoa powder in recipes since it has a quite different composition. Some of the low-fat types contain no cocoa at all, but chocolate-flavoured substitutes.

Chocolate-flavoured cake covering: is made from vegetable oil, sugar flavourings and cocoa and has a tendency to leave a fatty film in the mouth. It is not recommended for the recipes in this book.

COOKING WITH CHOCOLATE

Chocolate has two main qualities which make it such an attractive cooking ingredient: it rarely becomes rancid and it melts at 33–35°C/92–95°F, the temperature of the human tongue. The more cocoa butter there is, the creamier, richer and softer the chocolate will be: a good-quality chocolate melts evenly in the mouth.

Chocolate should always have a shiny appearance and smell fresh and break evenly, not crumble. It should not feel greasy or sticky. Chocolate that looks dull may either be stale or not contain enough cocoa butter in its composition, in which case it will probably be hard and brittle as well. Bitter chocolate has more flavour than milk chocolate, to which milk powder, sugar and other flavourings have been added, which is why dark chocolate is preferred by most gourmets.

MELTING AND TEMPERING CHOCOLATE

Melting: being high in starch, chocolate burns very easily, so great care should be taken when melting it.

If melting chocolate on its own, the best way is to use a bain-marie, or double boiler. If using a heatproof bowl over a saucepan of simmering water, make sure the bowl fits in snugly and that the hot water does not touch the bottom of the bowl or it will overheat the chocolate. Also, no steam should come in contact with the melting chocolate. Moisture will 'seize' the chocolate, making it granular. It can be rescued by adding clarified butter, vegetable oil or vegetable shortening in small quantities (a teaspoonful) and stirring over a low heat until the chocolate becomes smooth again. This is not a foolproof method, however, and may alter the final result of the recipe.

Another good way of melting chocolate is in the microwave. Break the chocolate into small pieces in a microwave bowl and melt at low temperature, checking and stirring at regular intervals to make sure the chocolate is not overheating.

If a recipe calls for chocolate to be melted with a liquid ingredient like coffee, water, milk or cream, the liquid should be put in together with the chocolate pieces before melting begins, in this way avoiding the danger of seizing. Some French cookbooks are adamant that chocolate should not be stirred until it has melted completely. Chocolate of inferior quality can be quite temperamental, so perhaps this is a good rule to follow.

Tempering: this process ensures a final glossy and shiny appearance to chocolate. It is done with couverture chocolate which has a high cocoa butter content. The chocolate is melted until liquid (46°C/115°F), allowed to cool by stirring on a marble slab nearly to setting point (27°C/80°F), and then remelted to a dipping or working consistency (32°C/90°F). The chocolate is then ready to be used in the making of confectionery, Easter eggs, covering cakes, dipping fruit, etc.

If tempering is not done properly whitish-yellow streaks of fat, called fat bloom, will appear on the surface of the chocolate when it sets. The fat bloom will not affect the chocolate taste but makes for bad presentation. Bloom can also appear when chocolate is stored at too high or too low a temperature (see below).

Tempering is usually done by professionals since it requires maximum surveillance, not only of the chocolate temperature, but also of the working environment (controlled humidity and temperature), equipment and speed at which to work. The result is a glossy, shiny, smooth and beautiful chocolate.

Storing: chocolate should be stored at a constant temperature, preferably below 25°C/78°F, to avoid the appearance of fat or sugar bloom. If kept at too high a temperature the fat in the chocolate will melt and rise to the surface, and when cooled form a white powdery bloom, very common in chocolates bought in hot countries. The bloom does not alter the taste or nutritional value of the chocolate but it is unsightly. If it occurs on cooking chocolate, melting will make the fat streaks or sugar powder disappear. The ideal way to store chocolate is to wrap it tightly or keep it in its original packing, and store in a dry, cool cupboard. It will keep fresh for up to a year.

Chocolate freezes and defrosts well. Freeze the chocolate in an airtight container and allow it to defrost in the same container; in that way the chocolate will reabsorb the moisture it gave off while frozen.

CHOCOLATE DECORATION

CHOCOLATE CARAQUE

Chocolate caraque or flakes are simple to make and keep well for up to 3 days if stored in an airtight container in a cool place. Caraque can be made using dark, white or milk chocolate.

110g/4oz plain chocolate, chopped

1. Place the chocolate in a heatproof bowl. Set it over (not in) a saucepan of simmering water. Stir until the chocolate is smooth and melted.

2. Pour the chocolate on to a cold work surface (a slab of marble is ideal). Allow to cool and harden.

3. Take a large sharp kitchen knife and scrape it across the surface of the sheet of chocolate, making a cigar-shaped roll. Repeat until all the chocolate is used up. If the chocolate splinters as you work, this means that the chocolate is too cold and it should be moved to a warmer temperature.

CHOCOLATE CASES

These chocolate cases are quite easy to make and they provide a wonderful presentation for sorbets, mousses or ice creams.

MAKES 6

225g/8oz best-quality plain chocolate

1. Break up the chocolate and place in a heatproof bowl. Set it over (not in) a saucepan of simmering water. Stir until the chocolate is smooth and melted. Do not overheat or the chocolate will lose its gloss.
2. Brush the melted chocolate thinly over the insides of 8 small paper cases. (It is easier if you make double paper cases by slipping one case inside another.) Repeat the process until you have a reasonably thick but even layer. Leave to harden, then carefully peel away the paper.

NOTE: These cases can be made up to 2 days in advance and stored in an airtight container in a cool, dry place.

CHOCOLATE SHAPES

170g/6oz best-quality plain chocolate

1. Break up the chocolate and place it in a heatproof bowl. Set it over (not in) a saucepan of simmering water. Stir until the chocolate is smooth and melted. Do not overheat or the chocolate will lose its gloss.
2. Fill a piping bag with some of the chocolate and snip the tip of the cone to make a small hole. Use the chocolate-filled bag to pipe small elegant shapes on a piece of greaseproof paper. Leave to cool and harden.
3. Tip the remaining chocolate on to a second piece of greaseproof paper. Leave to cool and, when almost hard, cut into shapes.
4. Use as required, to decorate desserts and cakes.

CHOCOLATE LEAVES

Use different types of chocolate (milk, dark and white) for a contrasting leaf decoration.

MAKES 20–30

110g/4oz best-quality plain chocolate, melted (see previous recipe)

1. Choose clean, dry, non-poisonous leaves such as bay or rose leaves. Using a pastry brush, brush the melted chocolate on to each leaf.
2. Leave to harden, then peel the leaf away to reveal a perfect chocolate replica.

NOTE: Chocolate leaves are useful for decorating cakes and puddings and will keep well in an airtight container in a cool, dry place for up to a week.

BASIC GANACHE

Created by the Parisian pastry chef Siraudin around 1850, ganache is a mixture of chocolate and cream, used mainly to decorate and fill cakes. It is the simplest of the chocolate icings to make and it can be made lighter by whipping the chocolate cream once it has cooled.

340ml/12fl oz double cream
225g/8oz good-quality dark chocolate, chopped
½ teaspoon vanilla essence

1. Bring the cream to the boil in a medium saucepan. Remove from the heat and add the chocolate and vanilla. Using a balloon whisk, stir until the chocolate is completely melted and the mixture is smooth and shiny.
2. Transfer to a bowl and cool until the ganache thickens and leaves a trail.
3. To make light ganache (or chocolate frosting): using an electric beater, whisk the cooled ganache until it holds soft peaks. Do not over-whisk or the ganache will become granular.
4. Use to sandwich cakes and biscuits and spread or pipe on top of cakes.

NOTE: The ganache will keep in an airtight container in the refrigerator for up to a week. The mixture can be melted over a low heat or in a microwave until soft and spreadable.

FRENCH GANACHE

French ganache contains larger quantities of chocolate and butter, which makes it richer and shinier than the basic ganache.

255g/9oz good-quality dark chocolate, chopped
190ml/⅓ pint double cream
55g/2oz unsalted butter, softened

1. Mix the chocolate and double cream together in a medium saucepan. Cook over a low heat, stirring constantly until the chocolate has melted.
2. Remove from the heat, transfer to a bowl and leave the ganache to cool to the consistency of a thick sauce without allowing it to harden.
3. Using an electric or balloon whisk, mix in the butter until thoroughly combined.

NOTE: This recipe makes enough ganache to cover a 22.5cm/9in cake. The ganache will keep in an airtight container in the refrigerator for up to a week. The mixture can be melted over a low heat or in a microwave until soft and spreadable.

WINE WITH DESSERT

by Richard Mayson

Wine used to be hide-bound by a set of hard-and-fast rules – white with fish, red with meat, that sort of thing! Over recent years there has been a welcome relaxation in the wine lore that has been handed down from book to mouth, generation to generation. Most contemporary wine and food books rightly urge their readers to be more experimental in matching different drinks with different dishes.

But when it comes to pudding, one rule still applies. In order to prevent the wine from tasting sour or tart, it should always be sweeter than the dessert. Unless you are particularly fond of a spot of gustatory masochism, this effectively precludes dry wines from the dessert course. A few authorities recommend pouring a dry red over strawberries, but then others advocate serving strawberries with a sprinkling of ground black pepper. Maybe strawberries are the honourable exception.

However, the golden rule that ties sweet wine to dessert need not prohibit the sort of 'trial and error' experimentation that makes wine drinking all the more enjoyable. Most of us have ready access to more and varied styles of wine than ever before. This book is therefore full of alternative wine and dessert combinations based on my research. Some pairings like Sauternes with Summer Pudding (see page 126) are conventional; others may seem rather more radical but no less successful. Chocoholics, myself included, often feel excluded from a glass of dessert wine; however, help is at hand in this book in the form of young vintage or LBV Port or Australian Liqueur Muscat. Coffee is rather more difficult to match but a rich Bual or Malmsey Madeira is an answer.

A number of simple considerations apply when matching any wine to food, which are taken into account in this book. Wines should generally be paired according to the following criteria:

Acidity: youthful, acidic wines cut through the richness of creamy desserts. Fruit pies and puddings tend to need fresh-tasting wines with good levels of acidity. Sweet wines with insufficient acidity tend to cloy and end up tasting dull and boring.

Body: the richness of a dessert should be balanced by the body and richness of the wine. A full-bodied, unctuous dessert wine will swamp a delicate dessert and vice versa.

Fruit: desserts with fruit should generally be accompanied by younger fruity wines.

Sweetness: the level of sweetness of the dessert should be matched fairly closely by the wine. Wines that are less sweet than the pudding tend to taste dry or tart.
Tannin: not a major consideration as most dessert wines are made from white grapes and have very low levels of tannin. However, the tannins in a young Vintage or Late Bottled Vintage Port can be the perfect counterpoint to desserts made with bitter chocolate.

Over recent years sweeter wines seem to have been something of a victim of the British and North American fashion for drinking dry. Indeed, sweet fortified wines like sherry and Madeira have been suffering from a long-term decline in fortune. There is nonetheless an ever greater array of dessert wine available as producers in the New World muscle in on the Old. France, Spain, Italy, Portugal and Hungary are home to the classic sweet wines like Sauternes, sherry, port and Tokay, while relative newcomers like Australia, California and South Africa are currently forging their own new classics.

There follows a brief guide to the wines that accompany the desserts in this book:
Alsace: a region in north-east France. The wines are generally dry but there are late-harvest sweet wines labelled 'Vendange Tardive' or 'Selection de Grains Nobles'. Wonderful with fruit tarts like Tarte Tatin.
Asti, Moscato d': a sweet, sparkling wine from northern Italy, which goes well with light desserts such as soufflés and crêpes.
Australia: the most famous sweet wines are fortified Liqueur Muscats from Rutherglen in northern Victoria which go well with chocolate desserts. Also botrytis-affected Semillons and unfortified Orange Muscat are good with rich puddings.
Austria: as in Germany, wines are graded according to sweetness: Auslese, Beerenauslese and Trockenbeeren-auslese. These are wines for fruit puddings.
California: Orange Muscat is perfect with caramelized fruit.
Champagne: sweeter wines labelled 'Demi-sec' go well with crêpes or soufflés.
Constantia: the sweet Muscat-based wine from the Cape province of South Africa is an ideal accompaniment for richer puddings.
Coteaux du Layon: a fine sweet wine from the Loire Valley in northern France made from the Chenin Blanc grape. The best wines come from the appellations of Bonnezeaux or Quarts de Chaume. Their highish acidity tends to favour desserts with fruit.
France: see Alsace, Coteaux du Layon, Muscat de Beaumes-de-Venise, Sauternes/Barsac, Vouvray.
Italy: see Marsala, Vin Santo, Moscato d'Asti.
Madeira: a fortified wine from the Portuguese island in the Atlantic. The sweeter styles, labelled Bual or Malmsey, go well with caramelized desserts or dishes with almonds or walnuts.

Marsala: a fortified wine from Sicily which is often used in cooking, especially for zabaglione.
Muscat: a grape variety producing sweet, aromatic wines: see Muscat de Beaumes-de-Venise, Australia, Moscato d'Asti, Valencia, Setubal.
Muscat de Beaumes-de-Venise: probably the most famous wine to be made with the Muscat grape. A versatile pudding wine that goes especially well with richer desserts.
Port: fortified wine from northern Portugal. Vintage or LBV Port goes well with chocolate desserts, Tawny Port (served lightly chilled) with dried fruit, almonds and walnuts.
Portugal: see Port, Madeira, Setubal.
Sauternes/Barsac: these are classic rich, luscious dessert wines from the Bordeaux region of south-west France which are perfect for creams and custards or fruit desserts. Lesser, relatively inexpensive wine from nearby regions include Cerons, Loupiac, Monbazillac Ste Croix du Mont, Premières Côtes de Bordeaux.
Setúbal: a rich, fortified dessert wine from south Portugal is made predominantly from Muscat. It is good with Christmas pudding.
Sherry: a fortified wine from Andalusia in southern Spain. Sweet Oloroso or Cream Sherry is an ideal accompaniment for ice cream or dessert with almonds or walnuts.
Spain: see Sherry, Valencia.
Tokay (Tokaji): an intensely rich, aromatic wine from north-east Hungary. Its sweetness is measured in puttonyos, from three up to six. Eszencia is the most concentrated, for the richest of desserts.
Valencia, Moscatel de: a good, inexpensive Spanish dessert wine made from Muscat. Drink it as an alternative to Muscat de Beaumes-de-Venise with richer puddings.
Vin Santo: a strong, sweet Italian wine, mainly from Tuscany. Drink with Tiramisù or sweet biscuits.
Vouvray: fine sweet wines labelled 'Moelleux' from the central Loire Valley in northern France. Their highish acidity tends to favour desserts with fruit.

SERVING DESSERT WINE

Fine dessert wines should be served cool but not over-chilled as this tends to mask their more delicate aromas and flavours. German Auslesen, Beernauslesen or Trockenbeerenauslesen are particularly sensitive to temperature and should not be served too cold. An hour or so in the refrigerator should be enough.

The port shippers who inhabit the warm climes of the Douro Valley in northern Portugal have taken to serving Tawny Port chilled, especially during the summer months. Vintage and LBV Port, along with Oloroso Sherry and the richer styles of Madeira (Bual and Malmsey), should be served at room temperature.

Some dessert wines will throw a sediment in the bottle. A white deposit (often mistakenly thought to be sugar or even particles of glass) is in fact formed from naturally occurring tartrates precipitating in the wine at low temperatures. Tartrates are completely harmless and should not be seen as a defect in the wine. Merely decant the wine carefully before serving – a clean coffee filter or tea strainer may help.

Vintage Port and LBV Ports labelled 'traditional' will also throw substantial amounts of sediment (known as the 'crust') as they have not been filtered prior to bottling. These wines should therefore be decanted before serving; a simple procedure which requires a steady hand and an eye for the sediment. Just stop pouring the wine into the decanter when first you see any sediment. If the decanting is carried out carefully, you should lose no more than a centimetre or so (about half a glass) of wine in the bottle. Decant the wine before a meal: if serving lamb, beef or game, the sediment from a bottle of port can be added to the gravy.

PIES, TARTS, PASTRIES AND PANCAKES

APPLE AND WALNUT PIE WITH CHEDDAR PASTRY

This unusual cheese pastry makes a superb combination with apples, pears or quinces.

SERVES 6

For the pastry
225g/8oz plain flour
85g/3oz butter, diced
30g/1oz lard, diced
1 tablespoon caster sugar, plus extra for sprinkling
110g/4oz mild Cheddar cheese, grated
about 6 tablespoons cold water

For the filling
5 Granny Smith apples, peeled, cored and thinly sliced
55g/2oz walnuts, coarsely chopped
55g/2oz soft light brown sugar
1 teaspoon ground cinnamon
a good pinch of ground nutmeg
2 tablespoons ground rice
30g/1oz butter, melted

For the glaze
1 egg
3 tablespoons milk

To serve
Greek yoghurt or whipped cream

1. Preheat the oven to 200°C/400°F/gas mark 6. Put a baking sheet on the middle shelf to heat.
2. Make the pastry: sift the flour into a large bowl. Rub in the butter and lard with the fingertips until the mixture resembles coarse breadcrumbs. Stir in the sugar and cheese and add enough water, mixing first with a knife, then with the fingers of one hand, to make a firm but not damp dough. Wrap and chill in the refrigerator for 30 minutes before using.
3. In a large bowl, mix the apples with the walnuts, sugar, cinnamon, nutmeg, ground rice and butter.
4. Roll out the pastry on a lightly floured work surface to a 35cm/14in circle. Do not worry if the pastry does not make a perfect round. Gently transfer the pastry to a baking sheet. Pile the filling on the centre of the pastry to make a 25cm/10in circle. Gently lift the edges of the pastry over the apples, leaving a circle in the middle with no pastry to cover.
5. Mix the egg and milk together and use to brush the pastry edges. Place the pie in the freezer for 15 minutes, then brush again with glaze and sprinkle with some extra caster sugar. Place the pie on the hot baking sheet and bake in the centre of the oven for 25 minutes. Turn down the oven temperature to 180°C/350°F/gas mark 4 and bake for a further 15–20

minutes, or until the pastry is golden-brown and the apples cooked.
6. Remove the pie from the oven and allow to cool for 15 minutes. Gently transfer the pie to a serving plate and serve lukewarm with Greek yoghurt or whipped cream.

Suggested dessert wine: SAUTERNES/COTEAUX DU LAYON

Suggested main course: Game, chicken or turkey

APPLE AND CURRANT CRUMB PIE

This is a more refined version of apple crumble. It looks wonderful and tastes great.

SERVES 6

200g/7oz flour quantity rich shortcrust pastry *(see page 100)*

For the filling
30g/1oz unsalted butter
900g/2lb tart dessert apples such as Granny Smith, peeled, cored and thickly sliced
55g/2oz dried currants
55g/2oz soft light brown sugar
3 tablespoons Calvados or other apple brandy
2 tablespoons ground rice or semolina

For the crumb topping
45g/1½oz butter
55g/2oz plain flour
55g/2oz soft light brown sugar
55g/2oz walnuts, roughly chopped

To serve
whipped cream

1. Preheat the oven to 190°C/375°F/gas mark 5. Place a baking sheet on the middle shelf to heat.
2. Roll out the pastry on a lightly floured work surface and use to line a 22.5cm/9in loose-bottomed flan tin. Chill in the refrigerator for 20 minutes, then bake blind for 15 minutes (see page 100).
3. Meanwhile, make the filling: melt the butter in a large sauté pan, add the apples, currants, sugar and Calvados and toss gently. Cook over a medium heat for about 5 minutes, or until the apples are just beginning to soften. Transfer the filling to a dish and allow to cool slightly.
4. Make the crumb topping: in a bowl, rub the butter into the flour with the fingertips until it resembles coarse breadcrumbs. Mix in the sugar and walnuts.
5. Sprinkle the pastry base with the ground rice or semolina and spread the apple filling on top. Spoon the crumb mixture evenly on top of the apples and bake in the centre of the oven for 40 minutes, or until the crumb topping is golden and the apples are cooked.
6. Remove the pie from the oven and allow to cool slightly before unmoulding on to a serving plate. Serve warm with lightly whipped cream.

Suggested dessert wine: SAUTERNES/BARSAC

Suggested main course: Roast chicken or beef

NORMANDY APPLE FLAN

This recipe has been taken from *The Observer French Cookery School* by Anne Willan of La Varenne.

SERVES 6

225g/8oz flour quantity rich shortcrust pastry (see page 100)
double quantity frangipane (see page 227)
3–4 ripe dessert apples

To finish
double quantity warm apricot glaze (see page 208)

1. Wrap the pastry and chill in the refrigerator for at least 30 minutes.
2. Preheat the oven to 200°C/400°F/gas mark 6. Place a baking sheet on the middle shelf to heat.
3. Roll out the pastry and use to line a 30cm/12in tart tin. Prick the base lightly all over with a fork, flute the edges and refrigerate again until firm.
4. Spread the frangipane evenly in the chilled pastry case.
5. Peel the apples, halve them and scoop out the cores. Cut the apples crosswise into very thin slices and arrange them on the frangipane like the spokes of a wheel, keeping the slices of each half apple together. Press them down gently until they touch the pastry dough base.
6. Bake the flan on the hot baking sheet near the top of the oven for 10–15 minutes until the pastry is beginning to brown. Turn down the oven temperature to 180°C/350°F/gas mark 4 and bake for a further 30–35 minutes, or until the apples are tender and the frangipane is set.
7. Transfer to a wire rack to cool. A short time before serving, brush the tart with the apricot glaze and serve at room temperature.

NOTES: Normandy apple flan is best eaten the day it is baked, but it can also be frozen. Just before serving, reheat to warm in a low oven.

If using red apples, they need not be peeled.

Suggested dessert wine: SAUTERNES/ VOUVRAY MOELLEUX/COTEAUX DU LAYON

Suggested main course: Game or pork

TARTE TATIN

Although upside-down fruit tarts are quite common, none has achieved so much fame as this one made by the Tatin sisters, who ran a hotel and restaurant in France early this century.

SERVES 6

For the pastry
170g/6oz plain flour
55g/2oz ground rice
140g/5oz butter
55g/2oz caster sugar
1 egg, beaten

For the topping
110g/4oz butter
110g/4oz granulated sugar
1.4kg/3lb cooking apples
grated zest of 1 lemon

1. Preheat the oven to 190°C/375°F/gas mark 5.
2. Make the pastry: sift the flour and ground rice into a large bowl. Rub in the butter until the mixture resembles breadcrumbs. Stir in the sugar. Add the egg and bind the dough together. Chill in the refrigerator while preparing the topping.
3. Melt the butter in a 25cm/10in frying pan with a metal handle. Add the sugar and remove from the heat. Peel, core and thickly slice the apples. Arrange the apple slices over the melted butter and sugar in the base of the frying pan. Sprinkle on the lemon zest.
4. Place the frying pan over a medium heat until the butter and sugar start to caramelize. It may take 15–20 minutes and you will be able to smell the change – it is essential that the apples get dark. Remove from the heat.
5. Roll the pastry into a circle 5mm/¼in thick, to fit the top of the pan. Lay it on top of the apples and press down lightly. Bake in the preheated oven for 25–30 minutes.
6. Remove from the oven and allow to cool slightly, then turn out on to a serving plate and serve warm.

NOTES: If you do not have a frying pan with a metal handle, cook the apples in an ordinary frying pan. Let the butter and sugar mixture become well caramelized and tip into an ovenproof dish. Cover with the pastry and then bake in the oven on a hot baking sheet.

This tart is classically made with dessert apples. At Leith's the tartness of cooking apples is preferred although early in the season these tend to become soft and pulpy.

Suggested dessert wine: SAUTERNES/ VOUVRAY MOELLEUX/COTEAUX DU LAYON

Suggested main course: Pork or lamb

CARAMELIZED APPLE, HONEY AND ROSEMARY TART

Aromatic rosemary, native to the Mediterranean region, is used mainly in savoury dishes. The combination with honey and apples is a particularly good one.

SERVES 6

For the pastry
170g/6oz plain flour
a pinch of salt
55g/2oz ground rice
140g/5oz butter, cut into pieces
55g/2oz caster sugar
1 egg, beaten

For the filling
110g/4oz clear honey
1 teaspoon rosemary leaves
a pinch of salt
900g/2lb cooking apples, peeled, cored and quartered

To serve
crème fraîche

1. Preheat the oven to 220°C/425°F/gas mark 7.
2. Make the pastry: sift the flour, salt and ground rice into a large bowl. Rub in the butter with the fingertips until the mixture resembles coarse breadcrumbs. Stir in the sugar. Add the egg and bind the dough together. Chill well in the refrigerator while preparing the filling.
3. Bring the honey and rosemary to the boil in a small saucepan. Boil rapidly for about 2 minutes, or until the honey starts to caramelize. Pour into a 20cm/8in moule-à-manqué tin, covering the sides and base.
4. Arrange the apples, round side down, tightly on top of the honey.
5. On a lightly floured work surface roll out the pastry to the diameter of the tin. Press the pastry gently on top of the apples, tucking any extra pastry towards the inside of the tin.
6. Place the tin on a baking sheet and bake in the centre of the oven for 30 minutes, or until the pastry is nicely browned.
7. Remove the pie from the oven and allow to cool in the tin for 2 minutes. Run a sharp knife around the pie to loosen the sides, then invert on to a serving plate. Let it stand for 3 minutes before gently lifting the tin from the pie.
8. Serve warm or cold with crème fraîche.

Suggested dessert wine: AUSTRALIAN OR CALIFORNIAN ORANGE MUSCAT/BUAL OR MALMSEY MADEIRA

Suggested main course: Lamb or pork

PEAR, BLACKBERRY AND GINGER PIE

Although there are more than five thousand varieties of pear throughout the world, apples continue to be the universally favourite fruit. This recipe also works well with a mixture of both apples and pears, but the delicate flavour of pear complements the taste of the ginger and blackberries particularly well.

SERVES 6

For the pastry
225g/8oz plain flour
a pinch of salt
1 teaspoon ground ginger
85g/3oz butter, cut into small pieces
55g/2oz caster sugar, plus extra for sprinkling
1 egg yolk
about 4 tablespoons milk

For the filling
285g/10oz blackberries, picked over
110g/4oz caster sugar
55g/2oz plain flour
5 firm pears, peeled, cored and not too thinly sliced
juice of ½ lemon
1 tablespoon chopped crystallized ginger
2 tablespoons semolina

To serve
crème Chantilly (see page 223)

1. Make the pastry: sift the flour, salt and ground ginger into a large bowl. Add the butter and rub in with the fingertips until the mixture resembles coarse breadcrumbs. Mix in the sugar and make a well in the middle.
2. Beat the egg yolk with the milk in a jug and pour into the well. Mix to a firm dough, first with a knife, then with the fingers of one hand. Turn on to a lightly floured work surface and quickly shape into a ball. Wrap and chill in the refrigerator for 30 minutes before using.
3. In a bowl, toss together the blackberries, sugar and flour. In another bowl, mix the pears with the lemon juice and crystallized ginger.
4. Cut off one-third of the pastry and reserve. Roll out the remaining pastry on a lightly floured work surface to a 5mm/¼in thickness. Use to line a 25cm/10in loose-bottomed flan ring.
5. Layer the pie: sprinkle the semolina over the bottom of the pastry case and put in half the pears. Put all the blackberry mixture on top and finish with the remaining pears. (The pie may look too full at this stage, but when it cooks the pears will sink.)
6. Roll out the reserved pastry to the size of the top of the flan ring and gently press over the pears. Crimp the top and bottom edges together and cut 4 vents in the pastry to allow the steam to escape. Chill the assembled pie in the refrigerator for 30 minutes to 1 hour.
7. Meanwhile, preheat the oven to 220°C/425°F/gas mark 7, and put a baking sheet on the middle shelf to heat.
8. Before baking, brush the top of the

pie with a little milk and sprinkle some extra caster sugar on top. Put the pie on to the hot baking sheet and bake for 15 minutes. Turn down the oven temperature to 180°C/350°F/gas mark 4 and bake for a further 25–30 minutes, or until the pastry is golden-brown. Remove the pie from the oven and allow to cool in the flan ring on a wire rack before unmoulding on to a serving plate.

9. Serve at room temperature or slightly warm with a good helping of crème Chantilly.

NOTE: The pie can be frozen at the end of stage 6 and baked from frozen.

Suggested dessert wine: MUSCAT DE BEAUMES-DE-VENISE/MOSCATEL DE VALENCIA

Suggested main course: A not too spicy curry dish

DRIED FRUIT AND PUFF PASTRY PIE WITH ORANGE AND CARAMEL SAUCE

SERVES 6

340g/12oz flour quantity puff pastry (see page 104)

For the filling
285g/10oz mixed dried fruit, roughly chopped
55g/2oz fromage frais
110ml/4fl oz milk
1 vanilla pod, split in half lengthwise
30g/1oz caster sugar
30g/1oz semolina
grated zest of 1 orange

For the glaze
1 egg yolk
2 tablespoons milk
a pinch of salt

To serve
orange and caramel sauce (see page 218)
Greek yoghurt

1. Preheat the oven to 220°C/425°F/gas mark 7. Place a baking sheet on the middle shelf to heat.
2. In a bowl, mix the chopped dried fruit with the fromage frais.
3. Bring the milk, vanilla pod and sugar to the boil. Scrape the vanilla seeds back into the milk and discard the pod. Add the semolina to the milk and cook, stirring, over a low heat for a further 4–5 minutes, or until thickened. Remove from the heat, add the orange zest and allow to cool slightly, then mix with the dried fruit and fromage frais.
4. Cut off half of the puff pastry and reserve. On a lightly floured work surface, roll out the other half to a circle large enough to line the base and sides of a 20cm/8in loose-bottomed flan ring. Line the tin and spread the dried fruit mixture on top.
5. Roll the remaining pastry to a circle large enough to cover the pie. Brush the edges with a little water and place the pastry, wet edges down, on top of the fruit. Press the edges gently to seal. Cut 3–4 small vents on top of the pastry to allow the steam to escape.
6. Mix together the egg yolk, milk and salt and use to brush the top of the pie. Chill well in the refrigerator for at least 20 minutes. Place the pie on the hot baking sheet and bake for 25–30 minutes, or until the pastry is golden-brown. Remove from the oven and transfer to a wire rack. Leave to cool for 10 minutes, then gently lift the pie from the tin and transfer to a serving plate.
7. Serve warm or at room temperature with the orange and caramel sauce and hand some Greek yoghurt separately.

Suggested dessert wine: SAUTERNES/ AUSTRALIAN OR CALIFORNIAN ORANGE MUSCAT

Suggested main course: Lamb or beef – this is a winter dessert

PRUNE AND APRICOT FRANGIPANE TART

SERVES 6

For the pastry
200g/7oz flour quantity shortcrust pastry (see page 100)

For the filling
110g/4oz no-need-to-soak prunes, stoned and roughly chopped
110g/4oz no-need-to-soak apricots, roughly chopped
3 tablespoons Calvados
1 quantity frangipane (see page 227)

To finish
double quantity warm apricot glaze (see page 208)
30g/1oz flaked almonds, toasted

1. Roll out the pastry on a lightly floured work surface and use to line a 22.5cm/9in loose-bottomed flan tin. Place in the freezer while preparing the filling.
2. Mix the prunes and apricots with the Calvados in a small bowl.
3. Preheat the oven to 200°C/400°F/gas mark 6. Place a baking sheet on the middle shelf to heat.
4. Mix the dried fruit and soaking liquid with the frangipane and spread the mixture evenly into the chilled pastry case. Place the flan tin on the hot baking sheet and bake in the centre of the oven for 15 minutes, or until browned. Turn down the oven temperature to 180°C/350°F/gas mark 4 and bake for a further 30 minutes, or until the filling is set.
5. Remove from the oven, transfer to a wire rack and allow to cool for 15 minutes. Remove from the tin, then brush the tart generously with the warm apricot glaze. Sprinkle with the toasted almonds. Serve at room temperature.

Suggested dessert wine: SWEET OLOROSO SHERRY/VIN SANTO

Suggested main course: Pork or lamb

DRIED AND FRESH APRICOT TART

SERVES 6

For the pastry
170g/6oz plain flour
55g/2oz ground rice
140g/5oz butter
55g/2oz caster sugar
1 egg, beaten

For the filling
200g/7oz dried apricots
140g/5oz butter, softened
85g/3oz caster sugar
1.35kg/3lb fresh apricots, halved and stoned

To serve
crème anglaise (see page 225)

1. Preheat the oven to 190°C/375°F/gas mark 5.
2. Make the pastry: sift the flour and ground rice into a large bowl. Rub in the butter with the fingertips until the mixture resembles coarse breadcrumbs. Stir in the sugar. Add the egg and bind the dough together. Chill in the refrigerator while preparing the filling.
3. Soak the dried apricots in hot water in a bowl for 1 hour. Drain and discard the liquid. Purée the apricots with 30g/1oz of the softened butter.
4. Spread the remaining butter on the base and sides of a 20cm/8in moule-à-manqué tin. Spoon 55g/2oz of the sugar over the butter.
5. Arrange enough fresh apricots, round sides down, in the tin to cover the base, packing them in very tightly. (It is important to arrange the first layer nicely because it is the one which will be uppermost once the tart is turned over.) Spread half the apricot purée over the fresh apricots and sprinkle with half the remaining sugar. Continue layering until all the ingredients are used up, finishing with a layer of fresh apricots.
6. Roll out the pastry on a lightly floured work surface to a circle about the size of the tin. Gently lift the pastry on top of the apricots.
7. Using a skewer, pierce the pastry all the way down to the tin to allow some steam to escape. Bake in the centre of the oven for 45 minutes, or until the pastry is well browned. Remove from the oven and leave to cool for 15 minutes in the tin over a wire rack.
8. Invert the pie on to a serving plate and leave for another 5 minutes before gently removing the tin. Serve warm or at room temperature with chilled crème anglaise.

Suggested dessert wine: SAUTERNES/COTEAUX DU LAYON/VOUVRAY MOELLEUX

Suggested main course: Barbecues, a pork dish

FOUR NUT TART

Intensely nutty and luscious, this is inspired by the nut tarts of Germany and Austria.

SERVES 6

For the pastry
285g/10oz plain flour
1 teaspoon baking powder
140g/5oz butter, softened
1 egg yolk
2 tablespoons cold water

For the filling
110g/4oz walnuts, roughly chopped
110g/4oz hazelnuts, skinned and roughly chopped
110g/4oz almonds, flaked
55g/2oz pine nuts
55g/2oz butter
140g/5oz soft light brown sugar
4 tablespoons clear honey
100ml/3fl oz double cream
4 tablespoons water

For the glaze
1 egg yolk
2 tablespoons milk

To serve
450g/1lb Greek yoghurt
½ teaspoon ground cinnamon

1. Preheat the oven to 180°C/350°F/gas mark 4.
2. Make the pastry: sift the flour and baking powder together into a bowl. In a second bowl, mix together the butter, egg yolk and water and mix well with the fingers of one hand. With the other hand, start adding the flour by stages, mixing the pastry until it is no longer sticky. If necessary, add a little extra flour. Cut off one-third of the pastry, wrap in clingfilm and chill in the refrigerator.
3. Place the remaining pastry in the middle of a 24cm/9½in loose-bottomed flan tin. Using the fingers of one hand, press the pastry over the base and sides of the tin. Prick the base with a fork and chill in the refrigerator.
4. Make the filling: scatter the nuts together in a roasting pan. Place in the oven for 10 minutes, or until lightly browned. Remove to a plate to cool.
5. Melt the butter in a large heavy pan. Add the sugar and honey and cook, stirring, until the sugar has dissolved and the mixture is smooth and foaming. Add the nuts, cream and water and cook over a medium heat, stirring constantly, for about 10 minutes, until the mixture is thick. Allow to cool slightly.
6. Oil a large metal spoon and use to spoon the nut mixture into the chilled pastry base. Press gently to make a smooth surface, then chill in the refrigerator.
7. Roll out the remaining pastry on a lightly floured work surface. Cut into 2.5cm/1in strips and place them in a lattice pattern over the nut filling. Press the edges so that they stick firmly.
8. Make the glaze: mix together the egg yolk and milk and brush the pastry

strips, being careful not to let it drip on to the filling.

9. Bake in the centre of the oven for 35 minutes, or until the pastry is golden-brown and cooked. Remove from the oven and allow to cool in the tin for 10 minutes before removing the tart from the tin.

10. Mix the Greek yoghurt with the cinnamon and chill.

11. Cut the tart into small wedges and serve at room temperature with the yoghurt.

NOTE: This tart can be made up to 2 days in advance and stored in a cool place, loosely wrapped in clingfilm.

Suggested dessert wines: SWEET OLOROSO SHERRY/BUAL OR MALMSEY MADEIRA

Suggested main course: A vegetarian or poultry dish

CARAMEL PECAN TART

SERVES 6

For the pastry
170g/6oz plain flour
½ teaspoon ground mixed spice
110g/4oz butter, cut into small cubes
about 1 tablespoon cold water

For the filling
310g/11oz soft dark brown sugar
225g/8oz butter
170g/6oz honey
55g/2oz caster sugar
370g/13oz pecan nuts, roughly chopped
4 tablespoons double cream

To serve
Greek yoghurt or crème fraîche

1. Make the pastry: sift the flour and spice together into a large bowl. Rub in the butter with the fingertips until the mixture resembles coarse breadcrumbs. Add the water and mix to a firm but not damp dough, first with a knife, then with one hand. Wrap and chill in the refrigerator for 30 minutes before using.
2. Make the filling: place the brown sugar, butter, honey and caster sugar in a large saucepan. Bring the mixture to the boil, lower the heat and simmer for 5 minutes. Remove from the heat, add two-thirds of the pecan nuts and the cream and mix well.
3. Preheat the oven to 200°C/400°F/gas mark 6.
4. Roll the pastry out on a lightly floured work surface and use to line a 20cm//8in loose-bottomed flan tin. Chill in the refrigerator for 20 minutes, then bake blind for 15 minutes (see page 100).
5. Turn down the oven temperature to 180°C/350°F/gas mark 4.
6. Spoon the filling into the pastry case and scatter the remaining pecan nuts on top. Bake in the centre of the oven for 25 minutes.
7. Remove the tart from the oven and allow to cool completely before gently unmoulding.
8. Cut the tart into thin wedges and serve with Greek yoghurt or crème fraîche.

NOTE: Alternatively the tart can be made in a Swiss roll tin, cut into diamonds and served as a biscuit. Walnuts can be substituted for the pecan nuts, with delicious results.

Suggested dessert wine: OLD TAWNY PORT/BUAL OR MALMSEY MADEIRA

Suggested main course: Salad, or a light chicken or fish dish

PECAN AND SWEET POTATO PIE

There are many varieties of sweet potato, the most common being the yellow-fleshed (Virginia) and the pink-fleshed (Malaga), both delicious. They are cooked in exactly the same way as ordinary potatoes.

SERVES 6

For the pastry
170g/6oz plain flour
a pinch of salt
85g/3oz butter, cut into small cubes
about 4 tablespoons cold water

For the filling
255g/9oz sweet potatoes, peeled, cooked and mashed
55g/2oz caster sugar
55g/2oz ground rice
1 egg, beaten
grated zest of 1 orange

For the pecan topping
150ml/¼ pint golden syrup
2 eggs, beaten
110g/4oz caster sugar
55g/2oz butter, melted and cooled
110g/4oz pecan halves

To serve
whipped cream or rich vanilla ice cream (see page 181)

1. Preheat the oven to 180°C/350°F/gas mark 4.

2. Make the pastry: sift the flour and salt into a large bowl. Rub in the butter with the fingertips until the mixture resembles coarse breadcrumbs. Add the water and mix to a firm, but not damp dough, first with a knife, then with one hand. Wrap and chill in the refrigerator for 30 minutes before using.

3. In another bowl, mix together the sweet potato purée, sugar, ground rice, egg and orange zest.

4. Roll the pastry out on a lightly floured work surface and use to line a 22.5cm/9in loose-bottomed flan tin. Spread the potato filling over the base and put it into the freezer while making the pecan layer.

5. Combine the golden syrup, eggs, sugar and butter in a bowl. Stir in the pecan nuts and mix well. Gently spoon the mixture over the sweet potato mixture. Bake in the centre of the oven for 1 hour 10 minutes, or until the filling is set. Remove the tart from the oven and allow to cool completely in the tin before unmoulding on to a serving plate. Serve at room temperature with cream or rich vanilla ice cream.

Suggested dessert wine: AUSTRALIAN LIQUEUR MUSCAT/SWEET OLOROSO SHERRY

Suggested main course: Roast chicken or turkey

LEMON MERINGUE PIE

A perennial favourite.

SERVES 4

For the pastry
170g/6oz plain flour
a pinch of salt
85g/3oz butter
1 teaspoon caster sugar
1 egg yolk
very cold water

For the filling
30g/1oz cornflour
290ml/½ pint milk
30g/1oz caster sugar
grated zest and juice of 1 lemon
2 egg yolks

For the meringue
2 egg whites
110g/4oz caster sugar
a little extra caster sugar

1. First make the pastry: sift the flour with the salt into a bowl. Rub in the butter until the mixture resembles breadcrumbs. Add the sugar.
2. Mix the egg yolk with 2 tablespoons water and add to the mixture.
3. Mix to a firm dough, first with the knife, then with one hand. It may be necessary to add a little water, but the pastry should not be too wet. (Though crumbly pastry is more difficult to handle, it produces a shorter, lighter result.)
4. Roll out the pastry and use to line a 20cm/8in flan ring. Chill in the refrigerator for about 30 minutes to relax (this prevents shrinkage during baking).
5. Preheat the oven to 190°C/375°F/gas mark 5. Bake the pastry case blind (see page 100) for 15 minutes. Remove from the oven.
6. Turn down the oven temperature to 170°C/325°F/gas mark 3.
7. Meanwhile, make the filling: mix the cornflour (which should be very accurately weighed) with 2–3 tablespoons of the milk.
8. Heat the remaining milk. Pour on to the cornflour paste, stir well and return the mixture to the pan. Boil for 2 minutes, stirring continuously. Stir in the sugar.
9. Remove from the heat and allow to cool slightly, then beat in the lemon zest and juice. Add the egg yolks.
10. Pour this mixture immediately into the pastry case. Remove the flan ring and return to the oven for 5 minutes to set the filling. Make the meringue: whisk the egg whites until stiff. Add 1 tablespoon of the sugar and whisk again until very stiff and firm.
11. Fold in the remaining sugar. Pile the meringue on to the pie. It is essential to cover the filling completely or the pie will weep. Dust with a little extra sugar.
12. Place in the oven for 5 minutes or until the meringue is a pale biscuit colour.

NOTES: Home-made (see page 88) or good-quality bought lemon curd makes a good alternative to the lemon custard filling.

When making a meringue mixture with a powerful electric mixer, add half the sugar when the whites are stiff. Whisk again until very shiny, then add the remaining sugar and whisk until just incorporated. If using a hand-held electric whisk, add the sugar a tablespoon at a time once the whites are stiff.

Suggested dessert wine: SAUTERNES/ VOUVRAY MOELLEUX/COTEAUX DU LAYON

Suggested main course: Grilled fish

CANDIED LEMON TART

A favourite of pupils and staff at Leith's School.

SERVES 6

170g/6oz flour quantity pâte sucrée (see page 102)

For the filling
4 eggs
1 egg yolk
200g/7oz caster sugar
150ml/¼ pint double cream
grated zest and juice of 2 lemons

For the glaze
1 lemon
150ml/¼ pint sugar syrup (see page 42)

To decorate
icing sugar

1. Preheat the oven to 190°C/375°F/gas mark 5.
2. Line a 20cm/8in flan ring with the pâte sucrée. Chill in the refrigerator for 30 minutes, then bake blind for 15 minutes (see page 100). Remove from the oven and leave to cool on a wire rack. Turn the oven temperature down to 150°C/300°F/gas mark 2.
3. Make the filling: mix the eggs and egg yolk with the sugar and whisk lightly until smooth. Add the cream and whisk again. Add the lemon zest and juice. The mixture may thicken alarmingly but do not worry.
4. Put the pastry case back on to a baking sheet and spoon in the lemon filling. Bake in the oven for 50 minutes, until almost set.
5. Meanwhile, prepare the glazed lemon zest. Using a potato peeler, pare the rind from the lemon very thinly, making sure that there is no pith on the back of the strips. Cut into very fine shreds.
6. Simmer the shreds in the sugar syrup until tender, glassy and candied. Remove with a slotted spoon and leave to cool on greaseproof paper.
7. When the tart is cooked, remove the flan ring and leave to cool. Then dust thickly and evenly with sifted icing sugar and arrange the candied shreds on top.

Suggested dessert wine: MUSCAT DE BEAUMES-DE-VENISE/MOSCATEL DE VALENCIA

Suggested main course: Pork or rabbit

LEMON AND LIME FUDGE TART

Wickedly rich and sweet, this tart tastes best the day after it is made and should be served well chilled.

SERVES 6

For the crumb base
110g/4oz plain flour
55g/2oz butter, cut into pieces
1 tablespoon icing sugar

For the fudge filling
110g/4oz unsalted butter
grated zest and juice of 2 lemons
grated zest and juice of 1 lime
285g/10oz caster sugar
6 eggs, beaten

To decorate
icing sugar

To serve
creme fraîche or Greek yoghurt

1. Preheat the oven to 200°C/400°F/gas mark 6.
2. Sift the flour into a large bowl and rub in the butter with the fingertips until the mixture resembles fine breadcrumbs. Stir in the icing sugar. Scatter the mixture evenly into a 22.5cm/9in round ceramic dish 5cm/2in deep, and bake until just brown. Remove from the oven and set aside. Turn down the oven temperature to 100°C/200°F/gas mark ½.
3. Meanwhile, make the fudge filling: melt the butter in a medium saucepan. Add the lemon and lime zest and juice. Mix in the sugar and cook, stirring, for about 5 minutes, or until the sugar has dissolved. Remove from the heat. Add the beaten eggs, pour the mixture into a blender or food processor and process for 5 seconds.
4. Pour the liquid on top of the baked base and place the dish on a baking sheet. Bake in the centre of the oven for about 1 hour, or until the filling is just set. Remove from the oven and allow to cool, then cover and refrigerate overnight.
5. Before serving, dust heavily with sifted icing sugar and serve with crème fraîche or Greek yoghurt.

Suggested dessert wine: MUSCAT DE BEAUMES-DE-VENISE

Suggested main course: A light fish or poultry dish

LEMON AND RASPBERRY CURD TART

This tart looks superb and tastes great. It takes a bit of time to make, but it is worth the effort.

SERVES 6
170g/6oz flour quantity walnut pastry (see page 103)

For the curd
3 large lemons
110g/4oz unsalted butter, chopped
285g/10oz granulated sugar
4 eggs, lightly beaten
140g/5oz raspberries
icing sugar

To serve
fresh raspberries
whipped cream

1. Preheat the oven to 200°C/400°F/gas mark 6.
2. Press the pastry with the fingers into a 20cm/8in loose-bottomed flan tin. Chill in the refrigerator for 30 minutes, then bake blind (see page 100). Remove from the oven. Turn down the oven temperature to 170°C/325°F/gas mark 3.
3. Make the curd: grate the lemons on the finest blade on the grater, taking care to grate the zest only, not the pith. Squeeze the juice from the lemons.
4. Put the lemon zest, juice, butter, sugar and eggs into a heavy saucepan or double boiler and cook over a low heat without boiling, stirring constantly, until the mixture is thick. Strain into a bowl and allow to cool slightly.
5. Mix the raspberries with 1 tablespoon icing sugar in a small bowl and crush with a fork. Push through a sieve to extract a thin raspberry purée.
6. Add one-third of the lemon curd to the raspberry purée and mix thoroughly. Pour the remaining lemon curd on to the baked pastry case. Using a small spoon or piping bag, make bold designs or patterns with raspberry-flavoured curd on top of the lemon curd.
7. Place the tart on a baking sheet and bake in the centre of the oven for 25 minutes, or until just set. Remove from the oven and allow to cool in the tin on a wire rack for 10 minutes, then unmould on to a serving plate.
8. Serve with a dollop of whipped cream and fresh raspberries.

Suggested dessert wine: COTEAUX DU LAYON/VOUVRAY MOELLEUX

Suggested main course: A not too rich main course such as grilled or roasted meat, fish or poultry. Ideal for an elegant summer dinner

ORANGE TART WITH GRAND MARNIER CREAM

SERVES 6

170g/6oz flour quantity sweet rich shortcrust pastry (see page 100)

For the filling
4 oranges, washed
1 quantity crème pâtissièré (see page 224)

For the glaze
4 tablespoons orange marmalade
1 tablespoon water

To serve
150ml/¼ pint double cream
1 tablespoon Grand Marnier

1. Preheat the oven to 200°C/400°F/gas mark 6.
2. Roll out the pastry on a lightly floured work surface and use to line a 22.5cm/9in loose-bottomed flan ring. Chill in the refrigerator for about 30 minutes to relax (this prevents shrinkage during baking).
3. Bake the pastry blind for 15 minutes (see page 100), then remove from the oven.
4. Grate the zest and squeeze the juice of 2 of the oranges.
5. Bring a medium saucepan filled with water to the boil. Add the other 2 whole oranges and simmer for 3 minutes. Remove the oranges and refresh under cold water (this will soften the skins). Cut the oranges into thin slices and remove the seeds.
6. Mix the orange zest and juice with the crème pâtissière. Spread evenly over the pastry case. Arrange the orange slices neatly in an overlapping circle on top of the crème pâtissière.
7. Bake in the centre of the oven for 35 minutes, then remove the tart and allow to cool slightly on a wire rack.
8. Heat the orange marmalade with the water and when liquid, strain. Brush the warm glaze gently but generously over the orange flan.
9. Lightly whip the cream and add the Grand Marnier. Chill.
10. Serve the tart at room temperature with a good dollop of the flavoured cream.

Suggested dessert wine: AUSTRALIAN OR CALIFORNIAN ORANGE MUSCAT

Suggested main course: Roast duck or a vegetarian dish

CHESTNUT MOUSSE TART WITH CRÈME ANGLAISE

Chestnuts contain very little fat compared to other nuts and they make delicious purées that can be bought sweetened or plain.

SERVES 6

For the pastry
200g/7oz plain flour
a pinch of salt
100g/3½oz butter, cut into pieces
1½ tablespoons icing sugar
1 egg yolk
about 3 tablespoons water
55g/2oz milk chocolate, chopped

For the mousse
3 gelatine leaves, or 15g/½oz powdered gelatine
290ml/½ pint milk
2 egg yolks
1 teaspoon plain flour
1 × 425g/15oz can of sweetened chestnut purée
2 tablespoons brandy
290ml/½ pint double cream

To decorate
2 tablespoons cocoa powder

To serve
crème anglaise (see page 225)

1. Make the pastry: sift the flour with the salt into a large bowl. Rub in the butter with the fingertips until the mixture resembles coarse breadcrumbs. Add the icing sugar. Mix the egg yolk with the water and add to the mixture. Mix to a firm dough, first with a knife, then with one hand. It may be necessary to add more water, but the pastry should not be too wet.

2. Roll out the pastry and use to line a 20cm/8in flan ring. Chill in the refrigerator for about 30 minutes to relax (this prevents shrinkage during cooking).

3. Meanwhile, preheat the oven to 190°C/375°F/gas mark 5. Bake the pastry case blind for 20 minutes (see page 100). Allow to cool, then unmould on to a serving plate.

4. Soak the gelatine leaves in cold water. If using powdered gelatine, sprinkle over a little water in a bowl and leave for 5 minutes until spongy.

5. Melt the chocolate in a heatproof bowl fitted over (not in) a saucepan of simmering water. Remove from the heat and allow to cool slightly. Using a pastry brush, brush the baked pastry case inside with the melted chocolate.

6. Bring the milk to scalding point. In a bowl, mix the egg yolks with the flour until well combined. Pour the scalded milk on to the yolks and mix thoroughly. Pour the mixture back into the pan and cook over a medium heat without boiling for about 8 minutes, until the custard is thick enough to coat the back of the spoon. Squeeze the water out of the gelatine leaves, if using. If using powdered gelatine, dissolve over a low heat without boiling until

clear. Do not stir. Add the gelatine to the warm custard and stir until dissolved.
7. In a large bowl, beat the chestnut purée with the brandy, then fold in the custard until thoroughly combined.
8. In another bowl, lightly whip the cream. Using a large metal spoon, fold the cream into the custard and chestnut mixture. Spoon the mixture into the baked pastry case, forming soft peaks. Chill in the refrigerator for 1 hour.
9. Before serving, dust heavily with sifted cocoa powder. Serve with crème anglaise.

NOTE: This tart should be made at least 6 hours, but not more than a day, in advance.

Suggested dessert wine: MALMSEY MADEIRA/HUNGARIAN TOKAY

Suggested main course: This is an autumn/winter dessert and great at Christmas-time

CHOCOLATE AND ALMOND TART

This rich and moist tart is not for weight-watchers!

SERVES 6

170g/6oz flour quantity pâte sucrée (see page 102)

For the filling
85g/3oz very good-quality dark chocolate, chopped
85g/3oz caster sugar
85g/3oz butter, softened
3 eggs, beaten
55g/2oz self-raising flour, sifted
55g/2oz ground almonds, sifted
a drop of almond essence

For the topping
55ml/2fl oz double cream
55g/2oz dark chocolate, chopped
55g/2oz flaked almonds, toasted

To serve
whipped cream or crème fraîche

1. Roll out the pâte sucrée and use to line a 20cm/8in flan ring. Chill in the refrigerator for 30 minutes.
2. Preheat the oven to 180°C/350°F/gas mark 4. Bake the pastry case blind (see page 100).
3. Place the chocolate in a heatproof bowl and melt over (not in) a saucepan of simmering water. Remove from the heat and allow to cool slightly.
4. Cream the sugar and butter together until pale and fluffy. Add the beaten eggs gradually and mix in the melted chocolate. Fold in the flour, ground almonds and almond essence. Spread the mixture into the pastry case.
5. Bake in the centre of the oven for 35–40 minutes, or until the centre of the tart feels firm to the touch. Remove from the oven and transfer to a wire rack to cool.
6. Meanwhile, make the topping: put the cream into a small saucepan and bring to the boil. Remove from the heat, add the chopped chocolate and mix until it has melted and the mixture is smooth and shiny. Allow to cool slightly before spreading evenly on top of the tart.
7. While the topping is still soft, scatter over the toasted almonds. Serve the tart at room temperature with whipped cream or crème fraîche.

Suggested dessert wine: YOUNG LBV PORT/AUSTRALIAN LIQUEUR MUSCAT/BUAL MADEIRA

Suggested main course: Fish or chicken

COCOA AND RASPBERRY FLAN

This is a great buffet party flan.

SERVES 6

For the pastry
100g/3½oz butter, softened
55g/2oz caster sugar
1 egg, beaten
140g/5oz plain flour
30g/1oz cocoa powder

For the sponge lining
2 eggs
55g/2oz caster sugar
55g/2oz plain flour, sifted
2 teaspoons cocoa powder
½ teaspoon baking powder
½ teaspoon vanilla essence

For the topping
3 tablespoons raspberry jam
1 tablespoon water
about 3 small punnets of fresh raspberries
icing sugar

To serve
lightly whipped cream

1. Preheat the oven to 200°C/400°F/gas mark 6.
2. Make the pastry: beat the butter in a bowl until soft, add the sugar and beat until pale and creamy. Add the egg a little at a time.
3. Sift the flour and cocoa together into the creamed mixture and work to a smooth paste.
4. Press the pastry on to the base and sides of a 22.5cm/9in loose-bottomed flan ring. Chill in the refrigerator for 30 minutes.
5. Bake the flan case blind for 15 minutes (see page 100).
6. Meanwhile, make the sponge lining: put the eggs and sugar into a heatproof bowl and set it over (not in) a saucepan of simmering water. Whisk steadily until the mixture is thick and mousse-like.
7. Sift the flour, cocoa and baking powder together and fold into the egg mixture. Add the vanilla. Pour the mixture into the baked flan case.
8. Bake for a further 10 minutes, then turn down the oven temperature to 190°C/375°F/gas mark 5 and bake for about 15 minutes, until the sponge feels firm to the touch. Remove from the oven and allow to cool completely before unmoulding on to a serving plate.
9. To assemble: melt the raspberry jam with the water. Sieve and brush the top of the flan generously with it. Starting at the edge, arrange the raspberries in concentric circles to cover the tart completely. Dust lightly with sifted icing sugar and serve with lightly whipped cream.

NOTE: The flan can be made without the raspberries the day before and kept covered in a cool place. Arrange the raspberries on top up to 5 hours before serving but dust with icing sugar at the last minute.

Suggested dessert wine: BUAL OR MALMSEY MADEIRA

Suggested main course: Almost any main course

DRIED FIG AND PEAR FILO TARTLETS

Inspired by the sweet and luscious Arab pastries, these tartlets are delicious warm and make a nice change from mince pies at Christmas.

SERVES 4

butter for greasing and brushing
425ml/¾ pint medium-sweet white wine
225g/8oz dried figs, halved
85g/3oz currants
1 bay leaf
1 vanilla pod, pierced all over with a skewer
grated zest and juice of 1 lime
1 tablespoon rose-water
2 firm pears, peeled, cored and cut into small cubes
8 sheets of filo pastry
30g/1oz caster sugar, plus extra for sprinkling

To serve
crème fraîche or Greek yoghurt

1. Preheat the oven to 190°C/375°F/gas mark 5. Put a baking sheet on the middle shelf to heat. Generously butter a 12-hole patty tin and chill in the refrigerator.
2. In a medium saucepan, combine the wine, figs, currants, bay leaf, vanilla pod and lime zest and juice. Cook over a medium heat for about 30 minutes, until the figs are tender. Drain the fruit, reserving the liquid, and discard the bay leaf and vanilla pod. Add the rose-water to the liquid and set aside.
3. Purée the fruit in a food processor or blender, adding a few tablespoons of the reserved liquid if necessary to make a thick purée with some texture.
4. Transfer the purée to a bowl and mix in the chopped pears.
5. To assemble the tartlets: brush each layer of filo pastry with melted butter to prevent it drying out and cracking. Layer 2 rectangles of 4 sheets each.
6. Using 8.5cm/3½in pastry cutters, press out 8 rounds of filo layers and press them into the buttered patty tin. Using a slightly smaller cutter, cut 8 more circles to be used as tops.
7. Divide the fruit mixture between the filo cases and gently press the filo tops over it. Brush with melted butter and, using a small sharp knife, make 2 cuts in each pastry lid. Sprinkle lightly with some extra caster sugar and place the patty tin on the hot baking sheet.
8. Bake in the centre of the oven for 20 minutes, or until golden-brown. Remove from the oven and allow the tartlets to cool for 3–5 minutes in the tin. Gently remove the tartlets from the tin, transfer to a wire rack and leave until lukewarm.
9. Serve with crème fraîche or Greek yoghurt drizzled with some of the reserved sweet wine cooking liquor.

Suggested dessert wine: SWEET OLOROSO SHERRY

Suggested main course: Roast lamb or grilled lamb cutlets

PUFF PASTRY NESTS WITH ORANGE AND CARAMEL SAUCE

This is a modern version of a classic French dessert called *puits d'amour* (literally 'well of love' – love nests). It is simple to make and a must for puff pastry lovers.

SERVES 6

340g/12oz flour quantity puff pastry (see page 104)
beaten egg, to glaze
3 teaspoons caster sugar
1 quantity crème pâtissière (see page 224)
1 quantity orange and caramel sauce (see page 218)
3 oranges, peeled and segmented

1. Preheat the oven to 220°C/425°F/gas mark 7.
2. On a lightly floured work surface, roll the pastry out 2mm/⅛in thick. Using a 6cm/2½in pastry cutter, cut out 12 circles. Place 6 pastry circles on a damp baking sheet.
3. Using a 5cm/2in pastry cutter, cut the other 6 circles inside, leaving a 'picture frame'. Using a pastry brush, dampen the edges of the frames and place on top of the circles on the baking sheet. Knock up the pastry sides and brush the frames with egg glaze (take care not to dribble the glaze down the sides or the pastry will stick together). Chill in the refrigerator for 30 minutes.
4. Bake for 15 minutes, or until the pastry is crisp and brown. Remove from the oven and leave to cool on a wire rack.
5. Preheat the grill to its highest setting.
6. Using a forcing bag fitted with a large plain nozzle, pipe the crème pâtissière into the nests, forming a little dome. Sprinkle the crème pâtissière with ½ teaspoon of sugar for each nest. Place under the hot grill for 1–2 minutes or until the sugar is melted and caramelized.
7. To serve: place the nests on 6 dessert plates and spoon a little of the caramel orange sauce on top of the crème pâtissière. Mix the orange segments into the remaining sauce and spoon some on the side of the nests. Serve immediately.

NOTE: The pastry nests can be made the day before and stored in an airtight container. The assembling of the nests without the caramel sauce can be done up to 3 hours in advance.

Suggested dessert wine: MUSCAT DE BEAUMES-DE-VENISE/ AUSTRALIAN OR CALIFORNIAN ORANGE MUSCAT

Suggested main course: Game or lamb

MILLEFEUILLES

Dating back to the nineteenth century, when the pastry layers were sandwiched together with jam as well as cream, millefeuille is a classic teatime favourite. It is also delicious for dessert served with a fresh fruit sauce such as apricot, pear or boysenberry (see pages 207, 209, 212).

SERVES 4–6

225g/8oz flour quantity puff pastry (see page 104)
225g/8oz strawberries, hulled and sliced
290ml/½ pint double cream, whipped
225g/8oz icing sugar, sifted

1. Preheat the oven to 220°C/425°F/gas mark 7.
2. On a lightly floured board, roll the pastry into a thin rectangle about 30 × 20cm/12 × 8in. Place on a baking sheet. Prick all over with a fork.
3. Leave to relax, covered, for 20 minutes. Bake in the preheated oven until brown. Remove from the oven and allow to cool.
4. Cut the pastry into 3 neat strips, each 10 × 20cm/4 × 8in. (Keep the trimmings for decoration.) Choose the piece of pastry with the smoothest base, and reserve. Spread the other 2 strips with cream, top with strawberries and sandwich together. Cover with the third, reserved, piece of pastry, smooth side uppermost. Press down gently but firmly.
5. Mix the icing sugar with boiling water until it is thick, smooth and creamy. Be careful not to add too much water. Coat the top of the pastry with the icing and, while still warm, sprinkle crushed cooked pastry trimmings along the edges of the icing. Allow to cool before serving.

NOTES: To 'feather' the icing, put 1 tablespoon warmed, sieved liquid jam in a piping bag fitted with a 'writing' nozzle. Pipe parallel lines of jam down the length of the newly iced millefeuilles, about 2cm/¾in apart. Before the icing or jam is set, drag the back of a knife across the lines of jam. This will pull the lines into points where the knife crosses them. Repeat this every 5cm/2in in the same direction, then drag the back of the knife in the opposite direction between the draglines already made.

Millefeuilles are also delicious covered with fresh strawberries and glazed with warm melted redcurrant jelly instead of icing the top.

Suggested dessert wine: MOSCATO D'ASTI/DEMI-SEC CHAMPAGNE

Suggested main course: Cold meat buffet

WARM NECTARINE AND FROMAGE FRAIS FEUILLETÉES

This recipe is equally delicious made with peaches or plums.

SERVES 4

340g/12oz flour quantity puff pastry (see page 104)

For the filling
200g/7oz fromage frais
85g/3oz icing sugar, sifted
½ teaspoon ground cinnamon
110ml/4fl oz double cream, lightly whipped

For the nectarines
6 nectarines, stoned and thinly sliced
55g/2oz caster sugar
juice of ½ lemon
55g/2oz unsalted butter, softened
icing sugar

1. Preheat the oven to 220°C/425°F/gas mark 7.
2. On a lightly floured board, roll out the pastry thin enough to cut into 8 neat rectangles 10 × 6cm/4 × 2½in. Place the rectangles on a damp baking sheet and prick all over with a fork. Cover and leave to relax for 20 minutes. Bake the pastry for about 15 minutes until brown. Transfer to a wire rack to cool.
3. Make the filling: in a large bowl, beat together the fromage frais, icing sugar and cinnamon until smooth and creamy. Using a large metal spoon, gently fold in the lightly whipped cream. Cover and chill in the refrigerator.
4. In a medium sauté pan, mix together the nectarines, sugar and lemon juice. Cook over a medium-high heat, stirring occasionally, for 5 minutes. Add the butter, stir well and continue cooking for a further 4 minutes or until the nectarines are soft but still retain their shape. Allow to cool slightly.
5. Heat 2 long skewers in a gas flame until red-hot. Leave them there while assembling the feuilletées.
6. To assemble: place 4 puff pastry rectangles on a work surface. Spoon some of the nectarines on top. Spoon the fromage frais mixture on top of the nectarines. Place the other pastry rectangles on top and press down gently.
7. Dust the tops heavily with icing sugar and brand a criss-cross pattern in the sugar with the red-hot skewers. Gently lift the feuilletées on to 4 dessert plates. Spoon any extra nectarines and sauce on the side. Serve immediately.

NOTE: The pastry can be baked the day before and stored in an airtight container. The fromage frais cream can be made up to 6 hours ahead and kept refrigerated. The nectarines can be prepared up to 6 hours ahead and reheated slightly before assembling the feuilletées.

Suggested dessert wine: SAUTERNES/ MONBAZILLAC

Suggested main course: Seafood, fish or veal

CHOCOLATE PROFITEROLES

These look spectacular piled high in a pyramid on the serving dish.

MAKES 30

For the profiteroles
1 quantity choux pastry (see page 105)

For the filling and topping
570ml/1 pint double cream, whipped and sweetened with 1 tablespoon sifted icing sugar
110g/4oz plain chocolate, chopped
15g/½oz butter
2 tablespoons water

1. Preheat the oven to 200°C/400°F/gas mark 6.
2. Put teaspoons of the choux mixture on a baking sheet, about 7.5cm/3in apart.
3. Bake in the preheated oven for 20–30 minutes. The profiteroles will puff up and become fairly brown. If they are taken out when only slightly brown, they will be soggy when cool.
4. Using a skewer, make a hole the size of a pea in the base of each profiterole and return to the oven for 5 minutes to allow the insides to dry out. Leave to cool completely on a wire rack.
5. When cold, put the sweetened cream into a piping bag fitted with a small plain nozzle. Pipe the cream into the profiteroles through the holes made by the skewer, until well filled.
6. Put the chocolate, butter and water in a heatproof bowl set over (not in) a saucepan of simmering water and leave until melted.
7. Dip the tops of the profiteroles in the melted chocolate, then allow to cool.

NOTE: If no piping bag is available for filling the profiteroles, they can be split, allowed to dry out, and filled with cream or crème pâtissière (see page 224) when cold, and the icing can be spooned over the top. However, made this way they are messier to eat with the fingers.

Suggested dessert wine: AUSTRALIAN LIQUEUR MUSCAT

Suggested main course: Beef or lamb

CRÊPES SUZETTE

This dish was created to honour the Prince of Wales's companion, in Monte Carlo at the turn of the century.

SERVES 4–6

12 French pancakes (see page 106)

For the orange butter
85g/3oz unsalted butter
30g/1oz caster sugar
grated zest of 1 orange
2 tablespoons orange juice
2 tablespoons orange Curaçao or Grand Marnier

To flame
caster sugar
2 tablespoons orange Curaçao or Grand Marnier
1 tablespoon brandy

1. Put the butter, sugar, orange zest, juice and Curaçao or Grand Marnier into a large frying pan and simmer gently for 2 minutes.
2. Put a pancake into the frying pan and, using a spoon and fork, fold it in half and then in half again. Add a second pancake and repeat the process until the pan has been filled. If the pan begins to look a little dry, add a little water.
3. Sprinkle the pancakes with caster sugar and pour over the orange Curaçao or Grand Marnier and brandy. Light a match, stand back, and light the alcohol. Spoon it over the pancakes until the flames have subsided. Serve immediately.

Suggested dessert wine: AUSTRALIAN OR CALIFORNIAN ORANGE MUSCAT

Suggested main course: Roast duck

SHORTCRUST PASTRY (PÂTE BRISÉE)

170g/6oz plain flour
a pinch of salt
30g/1oz lard
55g/2oz butter
very cold water to mix

1. Sift the flour with the salt into a large bowl.
2. Rub in the fats until the mixture resembles coarse breadcrumbs.
3. Add 2 tablespoons water to the mixture. Mix to a firm dough, first with a knife, then with one hand. It may be necessary to add more water, but the pastry should not be too damp. (Though crumbly pastry is more difficult to handle, it produces a shorter, lighter result.)
4. Wrap and chill in the refrigerator for 30 minutes before using. Or allow to relax after rolling out but before baking.

BAKING BLIND Line the raw pastry case with a piece of kitchen foil or a double sheet of greaseproof paper and fill it with dried beans, lentils, rice or even pebbles or coins. This is to prevent the pastry bubbling up during cooking. When the pastry is half cooked (about 15 minutes) the lining paper and 'blind beans' can be removed and the empty pastry case further dried out in the oven. The beans can be re-used indefinitely.

RICH SHORTCRUST PASTRY

170g/6oz plain flour
a pinch of salt
100g/3½oz butter
1 egg yolk
very cold water to mix

1. Sift the flour with the salt into a large bowl.
2. Rub in the butter until the mixture resembles breadcrumbs.
3. Mix the egg yolk with 2 tablespoons water and add to the mixture.
4. Mix to a firm dough, first with a knife, then with one hand. It may be necessary to add more water, but the pastry should not be too damp. (Though crumbly pastry is more difficult to handle, it produces a shorter, lighter result.)
5. Wrap and chill in the refrigerator for 30 minutes before using. Or allow to relax after rolling out but before baking.

NOTE: To make sweet rich shortcrust pastry, mix in 1 tablespoon caster suger once the fat has been rubbed into the flour.

SWEET PASTRY

This is more like a biscuit pastry. It is very easy to make and freezes well.

225g/8oz butter
110g/4oz sugar
2 eggs, beaten
vanilla essence
450g/1lb plain flour

1. Cream the butter well in a large bowl. Add the sugar and beat well until light and fluffy. Add the eggs a little at a time, until all is incorporated.
2. Add the vanilla, mix in the flour and mix thoroughly to form a soft dough. Cover and chill in the refrigerator before using.

NOTES: If using a food processor, cream the butter and sugar together, add the vanilla and flour and process until the dough just comes away from the sides of the bowl.

Chill the pastry well before using. If it is still too difficult to handle and roll out with a rolling-pin, use your fingers to press it into the flan ring. Chill well before baking.

PÂTE SUCRÉE

170g/6oz plain flour
a pinch of salt
85g/3oz butter, softened
3 egg yolks
85g/3oz sugar
2 drops of vanilla essence

1. Sift the flour with the salt on to a board. Make a large well in the centre and put the butter in it. Place the egg yolks and sugar on the butter with the vanilla.
2. Using the fingertips of one hand, mix the butter, yolks and sugar together. When mixed to a soft paste, draw in the flour and knead just until the pastry is smooth.
3. If the pastry is very soft, wrap and chill, before rolling or pressing out to the required shape. In any event the pastry must be allowed to relax for 30 minutes either before or after rolling out, before baking.

WALNUT PASTRY

This pastry can also be made using hazelnuts or almonds, both with delicious results.

170g/6oz plain flour
a pinch of salt
85g/3oz butter
85g/3oz ground walnuts
30g/1oz caster sugar
beaten egg

1. Sift the flour and salt into a large bowl. Rub in the butter with the fingertips until the mixture resembles coarse breadcrumbs. Mix in the ground walnuts and sugar.
2. Add enough beaten egg (probably half an egg) just to bind the dough together. Knead lightly. Wrap and chill in the refrigerator before using.

NOTES: If using a food processor, simply process all the ingredients together until they form a soft dough. Chill well before using.

If the pastry is too difficult to handle and roll out with a rolling pin, press it with the fingers into the flan ring and chill well before baking.

PUFF PASTRY

225g/8oz plain flour
a pinch of salt
30g/1oz lard
120–150ml/4–5fl oz iced water
140–200g/5–7oz butter

1. If you have never made puff pastry before, use the smaller amounts of butter: this will give a normal pastry. If you have some experience, more butter will produce a lighter, very rich pastry.
2. Sift the flour with the salt into a large bowl. Rub in the lard. Add enough water to mix with a knife to a doughy consistency. Turn on to a floured board and knead quickly until just smooth. Wrap and chill in the refrigerator for 30 minutes.
3. Lightly flour the board and roll the dough into a rectangle about 30 × 10cm/12 × 4in.
4. Tap the butter lightly with a floured rolling pin to shape it into a flattened block about 9 × 8cm/3½ × 3in. Put the butter on the rectangle of pastry and fold both ends over to enclose it. Fold the third closest to you over first and then bring the top third down. Press the sides together to prevent the butter escaping. Give it a 90-degree anti-clockwise turn so that the folded, closed edge is on your left.
5. Now tap the pastry parcel with the rolling pin to flatten the butter a little; then roll out, quickly and lightly, until the pastry is 3 times as long as it is wide. Fold it very evenly in 3, first folding the third closest to you over, then bringing the top third down. Give it a 90-degree anti-clockwise turn so that the folded, closed edge is on your left. Again press the edges firmly with the rolling pin. Then roll out again to form a rectangle as before.
6. Now the pastry has had 2 rolls and folds, or 'turns' as they are called. It should be put to rest in a cool place for 30 minutes or so. The rolling and folding must be repeated twice more, the pastry again rested, and then again given 2 more turns. This makes a total of 6 turns. If the butter is still very streaky, roll and fold it once more.

CHOUX PASTRY

85g/3oz butter
200ml/7fl oz water
105g/3¾oz plain flour, well sifted
a pinch of salt
3 eggs

1. Put the butter and water into a heavy saucepan. Bring slowly to the boil so that by the time the water boils the butter is completely melted.
2. Immediately the mixture is boiling really fast, tip in all the flour with the salt and remove the pan from the heat.
3. Working as fast as you can, beat the mixture hard with the wooden spoon: it will soon become thick and smooth and leave the sides of the pan.
4. Stand the bottom of the saucepan in a bowl or sink of cold water to speed up the cooling process.
5. When the mixture is cool, beat in the eggs, a little at a time, until it is soft, shiny and smooth. If the eggs are large, it may not be necessary to add all of them. The mixture should be of a dropping consistency – not too runny. ('Dropping consistency' means that the mixture will fall off a spoon rather reluctantly and all in a blob; if it runs off, it is too wet, and if it will not fall even when the spoon is jerked slightly, it is too thick.)
6. Use as required.

FRENCH PANCAKES (CRÊPES)

MAKES ABOUT 12

110g/4oz plain flour
a pinch of salt
1 egg
1 egg yolk
290ml/½ pint milk, or milk and water mixed
1 tablespoon oil
oil for cooking

1. Sift the flour with the salt into a bowl and make a well in the centre, exposing the bottom of the bowl.
2. Put the egg and egg yolk with a little of the milk into this well.
3. Using a wooden spoon or whisk, mix the egg and milk and then gradually draw in the flour from the sides as you mix.
4. When the mixture reaches the consistency of thick cream, beat well and stir in the oil.
5. Add the remaining milk; the consistency should now be that of thin cream. (Batter can also be made by placing all the ingredients together in a blender for a few seconds, but take care not to over-whizz or the mixture will be bubbly.)
6. Cover the bowl and refrigerate for about 30 minutes. This is done so that the starch cells will swell, giving a lighter result.
7. Prepare a pancake pan or frying pan by heating well and wiping with oil. Pancakes are not fried in fat – the purpose of the oil is simply to prevent sticking.
8. When the pan is ready, pour in about 1 tablespoon batter and swirl about the pan until evenly spread across the bottom.
9. Place over heat and, after 1 minute, using a palette knife and your fingers, turn the pancake over and cook again until brown. (Pancakes should be extremely thin, so if the first one is too thick, add a little extra milk to the batter. The first pancake is unlikely to be perfect, and is often discarded.)
10. Make up all the pancakes, turning them out on to a tea-towel or plate.

NOTES: Pancakes can be kept warm in a folded tea-towel on a plate over a saucepan of simmering water, in the oven, or in a warmer. If allowed to cool, they may be reheated by being returned to the frying pan or by warming in the oven.

Pancakes freeze well, but should be separated by pieces of greaseproof paper. They may also be refrigerated for a day or two.

FRUIT DESSERTS

BAKED APPLES

An easy, homely dish that can be made special served with warm caramel sauce (see page 217) and ice cream or Greek yoghurt.

1 smallish cooking apple per person
soft light brown sugar
sultanas

1. Preheat the oven to 180°C/350°F/gas mark 4.
2. Wash the apples and remove the cores with an apple corer. With a sharp knife cut a ring just through the apple skin about two-thirds of the way up each apple.
3. Put the apples into an ovenproof dish and stuff the centres with a mixture of sugar and sultanas.
4. Sprinkle 2 teaspoons sugar over each apple. Then pour 5mm/¼in of water into the dish over the apples.
5. Bake in the oven for about 45 minutes, or until the apples are soft right through when tested with a skewer.

Suggested dessert wine: VOUVRAY MOELLEUX/COTEAUX DU LAYON/GERMAN OR AUSTRIAN AUSLESE

Suggested main course: Roast chicken or lamb

APPLES IN CIDER JELLY

SERVES 6

6 Granny Smith apples, peeled, cored and cut into 2.5cm/1in dice
juice of 1 lemon
30g/1oz butter
55g/2oz soft light brown sugar
140g/4oz sultanas
3 tablespoons water
30g/1oz powdered gelatine
750ml/1¼ pints sweet cider

To serve
whipped cream or Greek yoghurt

1. Mix the apple dice with the lemon juice.
2. Melt the butter in a sauté pan and add the apples, sugar and sultanas. Cook over a medium heat, stirring gently, until the apples are beginning to brown but still retain their shape. Remove from the heat and allow to cool.
3. Put the water into a small saucepan, sprinkle over the gelatine and leave for 5 minutes until spongy. Dissolve over a low heat without boiling until liquid and clear. Do not stir.
4. In a large saucepan, gently heat the cider to just below boiling point. Remove from the heat and add the liquid gelatine.
5. Wet a 23cm/9½in jelly ring mould and pour in 6 tablespoons of the cider mixture, turning to coat the tin. Refrigerate for 10 minutes, until set.
6. Spoon the apple mixture evenly into the mould and gently pour the cider jelly over. Use a fork to make sure that the liquid is well spread between the apples. Cover with oiled clingfilm and chill in the refrigerator for at least 12 hours until set.
7. To unmould: loosen the top edge all round with a finger. Dip the mould briefly into hot water. Place a dish over the mould and invert the two together. Give a good sharp shake and remove the mould.
8. Serve well-chilled with whipped cream or yoghurt.

Suggested dessert wine: COTEAUX DU LAYON/VOUVRAY MOELLEUX

Suggested main course: Pork or game

SAUTÉD PEARS

This very simple dessert looks and tastes wonderful. To make it into something special, serve with rich vanilla ice cream (see page 181) or lightly whipped cream.

SERVES 4

4 firm, ripe pears, peeled, cored and quartered lengthwise
juice of 1 lemon
30g/1oz unsalted butter
55g/2oz caster sugar
3 tablespoons poire eau de vie (optional)
4 tablespoons single cream

To decorate
30g/1oz flaked almonds, lightly toasted

1. Toss the pears in the lemon juice.
2. In a sauté pan, melt the butter and add the sugar. Cook for 3 minutes, or until the mixture starts to colour slightly. Add the pears with the lemon juice and cook over a medium-high heat, turning only once when they begin to brown.
3. Add the *eau-de-vie*, if using, shake the pan in order to mix all the ingredients, and cook for about 8 minutes, until the pears are soft but still retain their shape.
4. Using a slotted spoon, gently transfer the pears to a warmed serving dish.
5. Using a whisk or fork, mix the cream into the sauce in the pan and stir until well blended and thoroughly heated. Pour over the pears and sprinkle with the toasted almonds.

Suggested dessert wine: COTEAUX DU LAYON

Suggested main course: Game or pork

SPICY PEARS

There is a saying, 'Peel an apple for a friend and a pear for an enemy'. This delicious dessert is for friends, none the less. Pears are usually peeled when they are to be poached.

SERVES 4

4 firm, ripe pears
8 cloves

For the syrup
150ml/¼ pint water
85g/3oz caster sugar
2 tablespoons clear honey
4 cloves
10 black peppercorns
1 cinnamon stick
1 × 2.5cm/1in piece of fresh ginger, peeled and sliced
thinly pared zest of 1 orange
290ml/½ pint Muscat wine
juice of ½ lemon

1. Make the syrup: in a large heavy saucepan, mix the water, sugar and honey and cook over a low heat until the sugar has dissolved completely. Bring to the boil, add the cloves, peppercorns, cinnamon, ginger and orange zest and cook over a medium heat, uncovered, for 10 minutes, or until slightly thickened and syrupy. Allow the syrup to cool slightly, then mix in the wine and lemon juice.
2. Prepare the pears: peel, leaving the stems on, and stud each pear with 2 cloves. Immediately submerge the pears in the syrup to prevent discolouring. Cut a piece of greaseproof paper to fit the diameter of the pan and place in the syrup.
3. Bring slowly to the boil, then reduce the heat and simmer very gently for 15 minutes. Remove the pan from the heat and allow the pears to cool completely in the syrup.
4. Lift the pears into a serving bowl and strain the syrup on top. Discard the flavourings. Refrigerate overnight and serve well chilled.

Suggested dessert wine: MUSCAT DE BEAUMES-DE-VENISE

Suggested main course: Beef casserole

PEARS IN RED WINE

SERVES 4

150ml/¼ pint water
290ml/½ pint red wine
110g/4oz granulated sugar
1 tablespoon redcurrant jelly
thinly pared zest of 1 lemon
a pinch of ground cinnamon or 1 cinnamon stick
4 firm pears

To decorate
30g/1oz flaked almonds, toasted

To serve
150ml/¼ pint double cream, whipped

1. Place the water, wine, sugar and jelly in a heavy saucepan and heat gently until the sugar has dissolved. Add the lemon zest and cinnamon.
2. Peel the pears very neatly, without removing the stalks. Place upright in the pan and cover with a lid. The pears should be completely covered by the wine and water mixture, so choose a tall, narrow pan. If this is not possible, wet the pears thoroughly with the mixture and turn them during cooking.
3. Bring the mixture to the boil, then simmer slowly for at least 20 minutes. The pears should be a deep crimson colour and very tender. The longer and slower the pears cook the better. (They can even be cooked overnight in an extremely low oven.)
4. Remove the pears from the pan and place in a glass serving bowl. Reduce the wine liquid by rapid boiling to a syrupy consistency, then strain it over the pears. Allow to cool, then chill in the refrigerator.
5. Sprinkle over the almonds just before serving and serve the whipped cream separately.

Suggested dessert wine: TAWNY PORT

Suggested main course: Vegetarian tart

SAUTERNES AND PEAR JELLY WITH PEAR SAUCE

SERVES 6

For the fruit
3 ripe pears
1 quantity sugar syrup (see page 42)

For the jelly
3 tablespoons water
45g/1½oz powdered gelatine
1 half bottle (375ml/11fl oz) Sauternes wine
300ml/9fl oz white grape juice
oil for greasing

To serve
1 quantity pear sauce (see page 209), chilled

To decorate
fresh mint leaves

1. Peel, halve and core the pears. Poach in the sugar syrup for about 20 minutes, until tender. Remove the pears from the syrup and drain well. Cut into 2.5cm/1in dice and reserve.
2. Make the jelly: put the water into a small saucepan; sprinkle on the gelatine and leave to stand for 5 minutes until spongy. Dissolve over a very low heat without boiling. Do not stir. When the gelatine is liquid and clear, mix with the wine, grape juice and pear dice.
3. Oil 6 ramekin dishes very lightly. Pour three-quarters of the jelly into the ramekin dishes, making sure that all the pears are used up. Chill in the refrigerator until beginning to set, then spoon over the remaining jelly. (This is to ensure that the jellies have flat bases when they are turned out.) Chill the jellies for 2–3 hours until set.
4. Unmould the jellies: loosen the top edge all around with a finger. Dip the ramekins briefly into hot water. Place an individual serving plate over each ramekin and invert the two together. Give a good sharp shake and remove the ramekin.
5. Spoon the chilled pear sauce around and decorate with the mint leaves.

Suggested dessert wine: SAUTERNES/ AUSTRALIAN BOTRYTIZED SEMILLON

Suggested main course: Duck, fish or foie gras

APRICOTS WITH MINT SAUCE

SERVES 6

900g/2lb fresh apricots
140g/5oz caster sugar
200ml/7fl oz dry white wine
3 tablespoons maraschino liqueur
12 fresh mint leaves, finely shredded

To serve
crème Chantilly (see page 223)

1. Halve and stone the apricots.
2. Mix the sugar and wine in a sauté pan and cook over a low heat until the sugar has dissolved completely. Bring to the boil, add the apricots and reduce the heat. Simmer gently until the apricots are tender but still retain their shape, about 10 minutes depending on how ripe they are.
3. Remove the apricots from the syrup with a slotted spoon and place in a bowl. Reduce the syrup by half by boiling rapidly. Allow to cool slightly, then add the liqueur and mint. Pour over the apricots.
4. Cover and chill in the refrigerator overnight. Serve well chilled.

Suggested dessert wine: MUSCAT DE BEAUMES-DE-VENISE

Suggested main course: Pork or lamb

NECTARINE AND KUMQUAT COMPOTE

SERVES 6

250ml/8fl oz unsweetened apple juice
190ml/⅓ pint sweet white wine, such as Muscat
30g/1oz soft light brown sugar
½ cinnamon stick, bruised
4 cardamom seeds, crushed
a pinch of ground nutmeg
4 black peppercorns
8 kumquats, cut into rings
4 nectarines, halved, stoned and cut into sixths

1. Put the apple juice, wine, sugar, cinnamon, cardamom, nutmeg and peppercorns into a large saucepan and simmer, stirring, until the sugar has dissolved completely. Increase the heat and boil for about 8 minutes or until the syrup is reduced by half.
2. Strain the hot syrup into a bowl and discard the flavourings. Add the kumquats, allow to cool, cover and refrigerate.
3. Just before serving, gently mix in the nectarines.

NOTES: The kumquats can be refrigerated in the syrup up to 2 days in advance.

The nectarines can be substituted by apricots, peaches or plums. If using peaches, they should be peeled.

Suggested dessert wine: MOSCATEL DE VALENCIA/MOSCATO D'ASTI

Suggested main course: A rich pork or fish dish

PLUMS BAKED IN RED WINE

The juice released from the plums during cooking mixed with the red wine make a delicious sauce, simply irresistible!

SERVES 6

900g/2lb firm plums
55g/2oz butter
85g/3oz soft light brown sugar
1 teaspoon ground cinnamon
150ml/¼ pint fruity red wine

To decorate
30g/1oz flaked almonds, toasted

To serve
cinnamon and vanilla ice cream (see page 182)

1. Preheat the oven to 180°C/350°F/gas mark 4.
2. Halve and stone the plums. Use half the butter to grease a shallow ovenproof dish large enough to hold the plums in a single layer.
3. Sprinkle the buttered dish with half the sugar and the cinnamon. Arrange the plums, cut sides up, in the dish in a single layer. Sprinkle with the remaining sugar, dot with pieces of the remaining butter and pour the wine all over. Cover tightly with a piece of kitchen foil and cook in the centre of the oven for about 25–30 minutes, or until the plums are just tender.
4. Remove the foil and gently tilt the dish to baste the plums with some of the cooking juices. Put the dish back in the oven, uncovered, for a further 10 minutes.
5. Remove from the oven and allow the plums to cool slightly. Sprinkle with the toasted almonds and serve warm with cinnamon and vanilla ice cream.

Suggested dessert wine: BARSAC/ COTEAUX DU LAYON

Suggested main course: Grilled meat

BAKED ORANGES

SERVES 6

butter for greasing
1 tablespoon cornflour
5 oranges
110ml/4fl oz golden syrup
1 egg yolk
1 tablespoon Grand Marnier (optional)
15g/½oz unsalted butter
1 tablespoon soft light brown sugar

To serve
crème fraîche or lightly whipped cream
pine nut sablés (see page 231)

1. Preheat the oven to 200°C/400°F/gas mark 6. Lightly grease a round shallow gratin dish with butter.
2. Grate the zest and squeeze the juice of 2 of the oranges and reserve.
3. Using a sharp knife, peel the remaining 3 oranges as you would an apple, removing all the pith. Cut into slices 1.5cm/½in thick and arrange in an overlapping circle in the gratin dish.
4. In a large bowl, whisk the reserved orange zest and juice with the cornflour. Add the golden syrup, egg yolk and Grand Marnier and mix thoroughly.
5. Spoon the liquid over the oranges and dot with small pieces of butter. Place the dish on a baking sheet and bake for around 30 minutes, until bubbling.
6. Meanwhile, preheat the grill to its highest setting. Remove the gratin dish from the oven and sprinkle the brown sugar on top. Place under the grill for 2 minutes, or until the oranges are slightly brown.
7. Serve warm with a dollop of crème fraîche or whipped cream and pine nut sablés.

Suggested dessert wine: AUSTRALIAN OR CALIFORNIAN ORANGE MUSCAT

Suggested main course: A spicy beef or lamb dish

Spicy Pears

Sauternes and Pear Jelly with Pear Sauce

Gratin of Oranges

Gratin of Summer Fruits

Caramel, Chocolate and Coffee Mousse Cake

Tropical Floating Islands with Praline

Coeurs à la Crème with Strawberries in Port

Pineapple and Coconut Soufflé

CRANBERRY AND DRIED FRUIT COMPOTE

The use of ginger and allspice gives this dried fruit compote an exotic flavour. It can be enjoyed well chilled on its own or with a dollop of fromage frais or Greek yoghurt.

SERVES 6–8

1 litre/1¾ pints cranberry juice
110g/4oz no-need-to-soak dried apricots, quartered
110g/4oz no-need-to-soak dried pears, quartered
110g/4oz dried figs, quartered
55g/2oz dried cranberries
4 tablespoons port
½ teaspoon ground allspice
½ teaspoon ground ginger

1. Combine all the ingredients in a large saucepan and bring to the boil. Reduce the heat and simmer for about 10 minutes, or until the fruit is tender.
2. Remove the fruit from the compote with a slotted spoon, place in a serving bowl and set aside. Boil the syrup for a further 8–10 minutes, or until shiny and slightly thickened. Pour the sauce over the fruit and allow to cool, then refrigerate until needed. Serve well chilled.

NOTES: Any combination of dried fruit will work well, just make sure to keep the same proportion of fruit and liquid.
Real maple syrup or good-quality honey can be substituted for the port.

Suggested dessert wine: TAWNY PORT

Suggested main course: Poultry

SUMMER FRUIT COMPOTE

SERVES 4–6

110g/4oz black cherries, pitted
225g/8oz strawberries
juice of 1 orange
juice of 1 lemon
2 tablespoons caster sugar
2 tablespoons Kirsch
225g/8oz raspberries
110g/4oz red cherries, pitted
110g/4oz blueberries
225g/8oz blackberries
225g/8oz loganberries

1. Process together half the black cherries, half the strawberries, the orange and lemon juice, the sugar and Kirsch. Taste and add more sugar if necessary.
2. Mix the remaining fruit together and pour the purée over it. Mix gently and pile into a serving bowl.
3. Keep the compote covered and refrigerated if not using immediately, but serve at room temperature.

Suggested dessert wine: SAUTERNES

Suggested main course: Barbecued meats and vegetables

FIGS POACHED IN RED WINE AND HONEY

SERVES 4–6

900g/2lb firm but ripe fresh figs
570ml/1 pint red wine
5 tablespoons clear honey
1 sprig of fresh thyme
1 cinnamon stick

To serve
tuiles amandines (see page 233)
lightly whipped cream

1. Gently pierce the figs with a skewer and set aside.
2. In a large saucepan, mix together the wine, honey, thyme and cinnamon. Bring slowly to the boil, then reduce the heat to a simmer.
3. Add the figs and simmer for 8–10 minutes, or until they feel soft and plump. Remove the figs from the syrup with a slotted spoon and transfer to a bowl.
4. Boil the liquid rapidly until reduced by half and syrupy and shiny. Allow to cool slightly, then strain the liquid over the figs, discarding the flavourings.
5. Cover and refrigerate for at least 12 hours. Serve well chilled with almond tuiles and hand some whipped cream separately.

Suggested dessert wine: YOUNG LBV PORT/AUSTRALIAN LIQUEUR MUSCAT

Suggested main course: Pasta or seafood

GRILLED FIGS

The figs can be served warm or at room temperature.

SERVES 6

12 fresh figs, halved lengthwise
port or sherry
55g/2oz soft light brown sugar

To serve
Mascarpone ice cream (see page 191)

1. Preheat the grill to its highest setting.
2. Arrange the figs, cut sides up, in a gratin dish. Spoon a little of the port or sherry into each fig and sprinkle with the sugar.
3. Place the gratin dish under the grill, getting the figs as close as possible to the heat. The sugar will melt and caramelize, so watch carefully, turning the dish so that the figs can brown evenly.
4. Allow to cool slightly and serve warm with the Mascarpone ice cream.

Suggested dessert wine: SWEET OLOROSO SHERRY

Suggested main course: A light main course

STRAWBERRIES IN PORT

Although strawberries are fairly common nowadays, being available throughout the year, a strawberry dessert gives an air of sophistication to any meal. This simple recipe makes the most of the natural delicious flavour of the fruit.

SERVES 4

450g/1lb strawberries
30g/1oz caster sugar
55ml/2fl oz ruby port

To serve
whipped cream
pine nut sablés (see page 231)

1. Wash, hull and halve the strawberries.
2. In a non-metallic bowl, mix the strawberries with the sugar and port. Toss well and leave to macerate for 2–3 hours.
3. To serve: divide the strawberries and juice among 4 tall glasses. Spoon a good dollop of whipped cream on top of each and serve with pine nut sablés.

Suggested dessert wine: YOUNG PORT/BANYULS

Suggested main course: A richer or heavier main course

STRAWBERRY AND RASPBERRY ALMOND TERRINE

This recipe is a little time-consuming but the result is a stunning and very delicious terrine.

SERVES 6

140g/5oz strawberries, hulled
140g/5oz raspberries
425ml/¾ pint full-fat milk
170g/6oz ground almonds
3 gelatine leaves or 15g/½oz powdered gelatine
5 egg yolks
110g/4oz caster sugar
5 drops of natural almond essence
225ml/8fl oz double cream, lightly whipped

To serve
raspberry sauce (see page 210)

To decorate
6 sprigs of fresh mint

1. Line a 900g/2lb loaf tin with clingfilm. Wipe the strawberries with damp kitchen paper and cut them in half. If necessary, clean the raspberries.
2. In a medium saucepan, mix the milk with the ground almonds and bring to the boil. Remove from the heat, cover and let the milk infuse for 2 hours. Sieve, discard the almond pulp and measure. If necessary, top up with some extra milk to make 425ml/¾ pint.
3. Put the gelatine leaves into a bowl and cover with cold water. If using powdered gelatine, put 4 tablespoons of water into a small saucepan, sprinkle the gelatine on top and leave for 5 minutes until spongy.
4. Reheat the infused milk to scalding point.
5. Mix the egg yolks and sugar in a bowl with a wooden spoon. Pour the milk on to the egg yolks, stirring steadily. Mix well and return to the pan.
6. Stir over a low heat for 8–10 minutes, until the mixture is thick enough to coat the back of the spoon. Do not boil. Squeeze the water out of the gelatine leaves and add to the hot custard, or dissolve the sponged powdered gelatine over a low heat without boiling until clear, then add to the custard. Stir until the gelatine has dissolved. Add the almond essence and transfer to a bowl, stirring gently until the mixture is on the point of setting, then fold in the lightly whipped cream.
7. Spoon one-third of the mixture into the prepared tin and place in the freezer for 5 minutes, or until the mixture sets slightly. Arrange a layer of strawberries on top and cover with another third of the cream. Place in the freezer for a further 5 minutes, or until set enough to support the weight of the fruit without sinking. Arrange the raspberries on top and spoon over the remaining cream.
8. Cover with clingfilm and chill in the refrigerator for 4–6 hours, or until set.
9. To serve: remove the clingfilm from the top and turn the terrine on to a

chopping board. Gently peel off the remaining clingfilm. Using a knife dipped in hot water, cut the terrine into thick slices.

10. To serve: place a slice of terrine on each dessert plate and spoon some of the raspberry sauce around it. Decorate with a sprig of mint.

NOTE: The terrine can be made up to a day in advance. If it is kept for longer, it gets a bit rubbery.

Suggested dessert wine: SAUTERNES/ AUSTRALIAN BOTRYTIZED SEMILLON

Suggested main course: A rich dish – this recipe is suitably refreshing to follow

SUMMER PUDDING

One of the classic English desserts, this tastes best made in summer with fresh berries, although frozen berries can also be used at any time of year.

SERVES 4–6

900g/2lb mixed redcurrants, blackcurrants, blackberries, raspberries and strawberries, or a mixture of just some of these
2 tablespoons water
170g/6oz caster sugar
6–9 slices of stale white bread

To serve
double cream, lightly whipped

1. Cook the redcurrants, blackcurrants and blackberries with the water and sugar in a saucepan for 5 minutes, or until just soft but still bright in colour. Add the raspberries and strawberries. Drain off most of the juice and reserve.
2. Dip slices of the bread into the reserved fruit juice and use to line a pudding basin.
3. While the fruit is still just warm, pour it into the bread-lined basin. Cover with a round piece of bread dipped in the fruit juice. Tip the remaining juice into a saucepan and reduce, by boiling rapidly, to a syrupy consistency. Leave to cool.
4. Stand the pudding basin on a dish. Press a saucer or plate on top of the pudding and put a 450g/1lb weight on top. Leave in a cool place overnight. Remove the saucer and weight.
5. Invert a serving dish over the bowl and turn both over together. Give a sharp shake and remove the bowl. Spoon over the reserved, reduced fruit juice. Serve the cream separately.

Suggested dessert wine: SAUTERNES/ BARSAC

Suggested main course: Poached salmon

GRATIN OF SUMMER FRUITS

This luscious dessert is served straight from the grill to the table.

SERVES 4

225g/8oz strawberries, hulled and halved
225g/8oz cherries, stoned
225g/8oz raspberries
55g/2oz macaroons (see page 234), crushed
2 eggs
85g/3oz caster sugar
1 tablespoon maraschino liqueur (optional)

1. Mix all the fruit together and arrange in 6 small gratin dishes. Scatter the crushed macaroons on top.
2. Preheat the grill to its highest setting.
3. In a heatproof bowl fitted over (not in) a saucepan of simmering water, whisk the eggs and sugar together for about 10 minutes, until the mixture is pale and thick. Add the liqueur, if using.
4. Spoon the sauce over the fruits and grill for about 5–8 minutes, until the mixture is evenly browned. Serve immediately.

NOTE: The recipe can be prepared up to the end of stage 1 and kept in a cool place until ready to cook.

Suggested dessert wine: SAUTERNES/ VOUVRAY MOELLEUX

Suggested main course: A not so rich poultry or fish dish.

FROZEN BERRY COMPOTE

Delicious in the summer or winter, this compote marries well with everything, from cakes to ice creams or simply whipped cream or yoghurt.

SERVES 6

450g/1lb mixed frozen berries
110g/4oz granulated sugar
225ml/8fl oz hot water
½ cinnamon stick
1 star anise
1 × 2.5cm/1in strip of thinly pared lemon or orange zest

1. Remove the berries from the freezer and leave to defrost for 1 hour.
2. Put the sugar, water, cinnamon, star anise and citrus zest into a saucepan and cook over a low heat until the sugar has dissolved.
3. Bring to the boil without stirring, then boil for 5 minutes, or until the liquid is reduced by one-third. Transfer to a bowl to cool. Remove the cinnamon, star anise and citrus zest and discard.
4. Mix the berries and juices with the syrup and toss gently. Chill well in the refrigerator before serving.

NOTE: This compote can be made up to 2 days in advance and kept covered in the refrigerator.

Suggested dessert wine: GERMAN AUSLESE/BEERENAUSLESE/ TROCKENBEERENAUSLESE

Suggested main course: Any rich main course

ARRANGED FRUIT SALAD

This light, refreshing dessert is a classic at Leith's School.

SERVES 4

2 ripe passionfruits
1 large ripe mango
3 tablespoons fresh orange juice
seasonal fruit, chilled, such as 4 kiwi fruits, peeled and sliced, 110g/4oz strawberries, hulled, 110g/4oz black grapes, peeled and halved
4 sprigs of fresh mint

1. Process (but do not liquidize) the passionfruit pulp, mango flesh and orange juice together for 2 minutes.
2. Sieve the purée on to the base of 4 dessert plates so that each one is well flooded.
3. Arrange the prepared fruit in an attractive pattern on each plate. Decorate each with a sprig of mint.

NOTE: If you do not have a food processor, the sauce can be made in a blender if the passionfruit are sieved before whizzing.

Suggested dessert wine: MUSCAT DE BEAUMES-DE-VENISE/MOSCATEL DE VALENCIA

Suggested main course: Fish or light pasta dish

DESSERT CAKES

CHOCOLATE CAKE

This cake is simple to make and not overpoweringly chocolatey or rich. It is particularly good served with a fresh fruit sauce or compote. The icing can be omitted and the cake simply dusted with sifted icing sugar.

SERVES 6

110g/4oz good-quality dark chocolate, chopped
70ml/5 scant tablespoons water
110g/4oz unsalted butter, softened
110g/4oz caster sugar
3 large eggs, separated
110g/4oz plain flour, sifted
2 tablespoons cocoa powder
1 teaspoon baking powder

For the tin
caster sugar, flour

For the icing
110g/4oz good-quality dark chocolate, chopped
30g/1oz butter
2 tablespoons clear honey
2 tablespoons milk

1. Preheat the oven to 170°C/325°F/gas mark 3. Grease a 20cm/8in moule-à-manqué or deep sandwich tin. Line the base with a disc of lightly greased greaseproof paper and dust lightly with caster sugar and then flour. Tap out any excess.
2. Put the chocolate and water into a small heatproof bowl and melt over (not in) a saucepan of simmering water.
3. Cream the butter well in a bowl, add the sugar and beat well until light and fluffy. Add the egg yolks one at a time, beating well after each addition.
4. Sift the flour, cocoa and baking powder together twice. Mix into the creamed mixture to make a fairly stiff mixture.
5. Whisk the egg whites until they form soft to medium peaks and stir 1 tablespoon into the cake mixture, to loosen it. Using a large metal spoon, carefully fold in the remaining egg whites. Pour the mixture into the prepared tin.
6. Bake the cake in the centre of the oven for 1 hour, or until a sharp knife or skewer inserted into the centre comes out clean. Remove from the oven and allow to cool in the tin for 10 minutes, then turn out on to a wire rack and leave to cool completely.
7. Make the icing: bring all the ingredients to a simmer in a small saucepan, stirring continuously. Cook over a very low heat until the mixture is smooth, shiny and thick enough to coat

the back of a spoon. Allow to cool slightly before spreading over the cooled cake.

NOTE: Without the icing, the cake can be frozen for up to 1 month and iced once it has defrosted.

Suggested dessert wine: AUSTRALIAN LIQUEUR MUSCAT/YOUNG LBV PORT

Suggested main course: Any main course – this is a good-with-everything cake

CHOCOLATE FONDANT CAKE

This is the famous 'death by chocolate' cake. For chocolate lovers there is nothing that can compare to it, complete indulgence. It tastes best if made a day in advance.

SERVES 6

oil for greasing
4 tablespoons water
110g/4oz sugar
255g/9oz dark good-quality chocolate, chopped
110g/4oz unsalted butter
4 eggs
½ teaspoon vanilla essence
30g/1oz self-raising flour

To decorate
cocoa powder

To serve
raspberry sauce (see page 210)
fresh raspberries and strawberries

1. Preheat the oven to 180°C/350°F/gas mark 4. Oil a 20cm/8in moule-à-manqué tin and line the base with a disc of greased greaseproof paper.
2. In a medium saucepan, mix together the water and sugar. Cook over a low heat until the sugar has dissolved completely. Off the heat, add the chocolate and butter and mix thoroughly until completely melted and the mixture is smooth and shiny.
3. In a large bowl, whisk the eggs and vanilla lightly. Add the chocolate syrup mixture and mix well. Using a large metal spoon, fold in the flour. Turn the mixture into the prepared tin.
4. Fill a deep baking dish with hot water (a bain-marie) and put the cake tin in the middle. Bake in the centre of the oven for 1 hour, or until the centre of the top of the cake is firm to the touch. Remove from the oven and leave to cool completely in the tin before unmoulding.
5. To unmould the cake: fill a baking dish with hot water. Quickly dip the bottom of the mould in the hot water for a few seconds, then unmould the cake on to a serving plate. Just before serving, dust heavily with sifted cocoa powder.
6. To serve: cut the cake into small wedges and serve with raspberry sauce and mixed raspberries and strawberries.

NOTE: This cake does not rise much.

Suggested dessert wine: AUSTRALIAN LIQUEUR MUSCAT

Suggested main course: A party dish. Not an everyday dessert, this makes a very good grand finale for a special occasion

CHOCOLATE CAKE WITH SPICY PEARS

This is a butter- and flour-free chocolate cake. It has a very light texture and the great flavour depends exclusively on the quality of the chocolate used.

SERVES 6

oil for greasing
110g/4oz bitter dark chocolate, chopped
4 eggs, separated
110g/4oz caster sugar
70g/2½oz cornflour

For the tin
caster sugar, flour

To decorate
icing sugar

To serve
spicy pears (see page 112)
whipped cream

1. Preheat the oven to 180°C/350°F/gas mark 4. Grease a 22.5cm/9in moule-à-manqué tin and line the base with a disc of greased greaseproof paper. Dust lightly with sugar and then flour. Tap out the excess.
2. Put the chocolate into a heatproof bowl fitted over (not in) a saucepan of simmering water. Stir until melted, then remove from the heat.
3. Beat the egg yolks with all but 1 tablespoon of the caster sugar until pale and creamy.
4. Whisk the egg whites until stiff. Whisk in the reserved sugar until shiny.
5. Mix the cornflour into the egg yolk mixture. Add the melted chocolate and mix thoroughly.
6. Using a large metal spoon, fold the egg whites into the egg and chocolate mixture and pour into the prepared tin.
7. Bake the cake in the centre of the oven for 20–25 minutes, or until the top springs back when pressed lightly with a fingertip. Remove the cake from the oven and allow to cool in the tin for 10 minutes, then unmould on to a wire rack and leave to cool completely.
8. Dust lightly with sifted icing sugar just before serving. Serve with chilled spicy pears and hand some whipped cream separately.

Suggested dessert wine: YOUNG VINTAGE OR LBV PORT/ AUSTRALIAN LIQUEUR MUSCAT

Suggested main course: A quite rich main course if this light dessert is served without the cream

CHOCOLATE ROULADE

This deliciously moist roulade can be filled with soft fruit, such as raspberries and strawberries, as well as cream.

SERVES 6

225g/8oz plain chocolate, roughly chopped
85ml/3fl oz water
1 teaspoon strong instant coffee powder
5 eggs, separated
140g/5oz caster sugar
200ml/⅓ pint double cream
icing sugar

For the tin
oil, flour, caster sugar

1. Take a large roasting pan and cut a double layer of silicone baking paper slightly bigger than it. Lay the paper in the pan; don't worry if the edges stick up untidily round the sides. Brush the paper lightly with oil and sprinkle with flour and then caster sugar. Preheat the oven to 200°C/400°F/gas mark 6.
2. Put the chocolate, water and coffee into a heavy saucepan and melt over a low heat.
3. Beat the egg yolks and the caster sugar until pale and mousse-like. Add the melted chocolate.
4. Whisk the whites until stiff but not dry. With a large metal spoon, stir a small amount thoroughly into the chocolate mixture, to loosen it. Fold the remaining whites in gently. Spread the mixture evenly on the baking paper.
5. Bake in the preheated oven for about 12 minutes until the top is slightly browned and firm to touch.
6. Slide the cake and paper out of the roasting pan on to a wire rack. Cover immediately with a damp tea-towel (to prevent the cake from cracking) and leave to cool.
7. Whip the cream and spread it evenly over the cake. Roll up like a Swiss roll, removing the paper as you go. Put the roll on to a serving dish and, just before serving, sift a little icing sugar over the top.

NOTES: The cake is very moist and inclined to break apart. But it doesn't matter. Just stick it together with the cream when rolling up. The last-minute sifted icing sugar will do wonders for the appearance.

If this cake is used as a Yule log the tendency to crack is a positive advantage: do not cover with a tea-towel when leaving to cool. Before filling, flip the whole flat cake over on to a tea-towel. Carefully peel off the lining paper, then fill with cream and roll up. The surface will crack very like the bark of a tree. Sprigs of holly or marzipan toadstools help to give a festive look. A dusting of icing sugar will look like snow.

Suggested dessert wine: AUSTRALIAN LIQUEUR MUSCAT/YOUNG LBV PORT

Suggested main course: Fish or veal

FROZEN CHOCOLATE MOUSSE CAKE

From the time chocolate was brought to Europe from the New World in the sixteenth century until over 100 years ago, it was only consumed as a drink. The chocolate confectionery industry was not established until 1850. This recipe, a combination of cake and mousse, looks and tastes fantastic and is very simple to make.

SERVES 6–8

55g/2oz unsalted butter, softened
110g/4oz caster sugar
6 eggs, separated
200g/7oz dark chocolate, chopped
1 teaspoon coffee granules
2 tablespoons water
225ml/8fl oz double cream

To decorate
cocoa powder

1. Preheat the oven to 190°C/375°F/gas mark 5. Grease an 18cm/7in springform tin 5cm/2in deep and line the base with a disc of greased greaseproof paper.
2. Beat the butter and all but 1 tablespoon of the sugar until pale and light. Add the egg yolks and mix thoroughly.
3. Put the chocolate, coffee and water into a heatproof bowl fitted over (not in) a saucepan of simmering water. Stir until melted, then remove from the heat and leave to cool slightly.
4. Add the melted chocolate to the butter and egg mixture and mix well.
5. Whisk the egg whites until stiff but not dry, add the remaining sugar and whisk until shiny and stiff. Gently fold the egg whites into the chocolate mixture.
6. Turn one-third of the mixture into the prepared tin and bake in the centre of the oven for 30–35 minutes, or until a skewer inserted into the centre of the cake comes out clean. This thin cake layer will serve as the base for the mousse.
7. While the cake is baking, lightly whip the cream, fold into the remaining cake mixture and chill in the refrigerator.
8. Remove the cake from the oven and allow to cool completely in the tin. When the cake is cold, spoon the chocolate/cream mixture on top. Spread evenly with a palette knife and freeze for a minimum of 24 hours. The cake can be made up a week in advance.
9. 30 minutes before serving, remove the cake from the freezer and run a knife dipped in hot water around the edges. Gently release the base of the tin and transfer the cake to a serving plate. Dust the top heavily with sifted cocoa powder.

Suggested dessert wine: AUSTRALIAN LIQUEUR MUSCAT

Suggested main course: A light and not too rich dish

ALMOND AND CHOCOLATE FUDGE CAKE

Rich and dense, this cake does not use wheat flour and keeps well for a few days.

SERVES 6

200g/7oz unsalted butter, softened
200g/7oz caster sugar
4 eggs, beaten
140g/5oz dark chocolate, chopped
85g/3oz ground almonds
55g/2oz rice flour
1 teaspoon baking powder

For the tin
caster sugar, flour

To decorate
icing sugar
chocolate leaves (see page 59)

To serve
frozen berry compote (see page 128)

1. Preheat the oven to 190°C/375°F/gas mark 5. Grease a 22.5cm/9in cake tin and line the base with a disc of greased greaseproof paper. Dust lightly with sugar and then flour. Tap out the excess.
2. Cream the butter in a bowl. Beat in the caster sugar until light and fluffy. Add the eggs gradually, beating well after each addition. Add a little of the rice flour if necessary to prevent the mixture from curdling.
3. Put the chocolate into a heatproof bowl fitted over (not in) a saucepan of simmering water. Stir until melted, then remove from the heat and allow to cool slightly.
4. Mix together the ground almonds, rice flour and baking powder and mix into the creamed mixture.
5. Gently mix in the melted chocolate until well combined. Spread into the prepared tin. Bake in the centre of the oven for 55 minutes, or until a skewer inserted in the centre comes out clean. Remove the cake from the oven and allow to cool completely in the tin.
6. Turn the cake out on to a serving plate and before serving dust heavily with sifted icing sugar and decorate with chocolate leaves. Serve small wedges of the cake with berry compote.

NOTE: This cake does not rise very much.

Suggested dessert wine: LBV PORT/ BUAL OR MALMSEY MADEIRA

Suggested main course: Salad or other light summer dish

STICKY PEAR AND CHOCOLATE CAKE

This cake was a great success with the Leith's staff when the recipe was tested. It is deliciously rich and moist.

SERVES 6

oil for greasing
285g/10oz good-quality dark chocolate
125g/4½oz butter, cut into pieces
2 eggs
85g/3oz caster sugar
1½ teaspoons vanilla essence
1 tablespoon strong black coffee
85g/3oz self-raising flour
85g/3oz pecan nuts, roughly chopped
675g/1½lb ripe fresh pears or 1 × 400g/14oz can of pears

To serve
crème anglaise (see page 225)

1. Preheat the oven to 190°C/375°F/gas mark 5. Grease a 24cm/9½in square ceramic or glass ovenproof serving dish.
2. Break up 200g/7oz of the chocolate and place in a heatproof bowl fitted over (not in) a saucepan of simmering water. Stir until melted, then stir in the butter piece by piece until the mixture is smooth. Allow to cool slightly. Chop the remaining chocolate into small pieces and reserve.
3. In a large bowl, beat together the eggs, sugar, vanilla and coffee. Mix in the melted chocolate. Gently mix in the flour, pecan nuts and the chopped chocolate until thoroughly combined.
4. If using fresh pears, halve, peel and core them. If using canned pears, drain and discard the syrup. Arrange the pears cut side down in the oiled dish and spoon the chocolate mixture on top. Spread evenly with a spatula.
5. Bake in the centre of the oven for 35 minutes, cover with kitchen foil and continue baking for a further 35 minutes (the centre of the cake should be moist). Remove the cake from the oven and cover with a damp clean tea-towel or kitchen paper (this will prevent the top from drying out) and allow to cool slightly.
6. Serve warm with chilled crème anglaise.

NOTE: The cake can be made a day in advance and reheated for 10 minutes in the oven preheated to 180°C/350°F/gas mark 4.

Suggested dessert wine: YOUNG LBV PORT

Suggested main course: Fish or veal

PETITS CARRÉS AU CHOCOLAT WITH STRAWBERRIES IN PORT

These intensely rich and quite sweet 'little squares' can also be served as petits fours.

SERVES 6

oil for greasing
140g/5oz butter, softened
140g/5oz caster sugar
3 eggs, separated
140g/5oz cocoa powder
140g/5oz plain flour
110ml/4fl oz milk

For the icing
225g/8oz caster sugar
½ teaspoon vanilla essence
4 tablespoons water

To serve
strawberries in port (see page 123)
sprigs of fresh mint

1. Preheat the oven to 190°C/375°F/gas mark 5. Grease a 20cm/8in square cake tin and line the base with a piece of greased greaseproof paper.
2. Cream the butter well in a large bowl, add the sugar and beat well until light and fluffy. Add the egg yolks one at a time, beating well after each addition.
3. Sift the cocoa and flour together twice. Mix tablespoons of the flour and cocoa into the creamed mixture, alternating with tablespoons of the milk until all the flour is incorporated.
4. Whisk the egg whites until they form medium peaks and stir 1 tablespoon into the cake mixture, to loosen it. Using a large metal spoon, carefully fold in the remaining egg whites. Pour into the prepared tin.
5. Bake the cake in the centre of the oven for 45 minutes, or until a sharp knife or skewer inserted into the centre of the cake comes out clean (the cake does not rise very much). Remove from the oven and allow to cool in the tin for 10 minutes.
6. Meanwhile, make the icing: mix together the sugar, vanilla and water to form a fairly stiff mixture. While the cake is still warm, spread the icing evenly on top with a palette knife and allow to cool completely (it will set to form a crust) before cutting into 5cm/2in squares.
7. To serve: place 2–3 squares on each individual serving plate and spoon a generous portion of the strawberries in port around. Decorate with a sprig of mint.

NOTE: This cake keeps well in an airtight container for up to 2 days. Without the icing it can be frozen for up to 2 months.

Suggested dessert wine: YOUNG LBV PORT/AUSTRALIAN LIQUEUR MUSCAT

Suggested main course: Veal, beef or lamb

CHOCOLATE PRUNIES WITH WARM CARAMEL SAUCE

These are deliciously chewy brownies with the butter replaced by a prune purée. They are best made a day in advance.

SERVES 6

butter for greasing
310g/11oz prunes, stoned and roughly chopped
150ml/¼ pint hot Earl Grey tea, strained
250g/9oz good-quality dark chocolate, chopped
150ml/¼ pint water
85g/3oz soft dark brown sugar
a good pinch of salt
110g/4oz self-raising flour
6 egg whites
85g/3oz caster sugar
a handful of flaked almonds

To serve
warm caramel sauce (see page 217)

1. Preheat the oven to 180°C/350°F/gas mark 4. Grease a 20cm/8in square cake tin and line the base with a piece of greased greaseproof paper.
2. Soak the prunes in the hot tea until the tea is cold and the prunes are soft, then purée with the liquid in a food processor or blender.
3. Melt the chocolate carefully in a heatproof bowl fitted over (not in) a saucepan of simmering water.
4. In a large bowl, combine the prune purée, water, brown sugar, salt and flour and mix thoroughly. Mix in the melted chocolate.
5. Whisk the egg whites until stiff, then slowly whisk in the caster sugar. Whisk until the meringue is shiny and thick. Using a large metal spoon, fold carefully into the prune mixture. Pour into the prepared cake tin and sprinkle with the flaked almonds.
6. Bake in the centre of the oven for 30 minutes, or until firm to the touch. Remove the cake from the oven and leave in the tin to cool completely. When cold, cut into 5cm/2in squares.
7. To serve: place a piece of chocolate prunie on each individual serving plate, add a dollop of whipped cream and drizzle everything generously with the warm caramel sauce. Serve immediately.

Suggested dessert wine: YOUNG LBV PORT/AUSTRALIAN LIQUEUR MUSCAT

Suggested main course: Lamb, pork or a vegetarian dish

CARAMEL, CHOCOLATE AND COFFEE MOUSSE CAKE

SERVES 6

For the base
1 chocolate cake (see page 136)

For the syrup
5 tablespoons strong, freshly brewed coffee
2 tablespoons Tia Maria, Kahlua or other coffee liqueur

For the caramel mousse
15g/½oz powdered gelatine
10 tablespoons water
a squeeze of lemon juice
170g/6oz granulated sugar
3 eggs
45g/1½oz caster sugar
150ml/¼ pint double cream

To decorate
cocoa powder and chocolate shavings

1. Bake the bitter chocolate cake mixture in a 20cm/8in deep loose-bottomed cake tin, as described in the recipe. Remove from the tin, invert on to a wire rack and leave to cool.
2. Mix together the black coffee and liqueur.
3. Wash the cake tin and oil its sides. Place a disc of greased greaseproof paper in the base. Split the cake in half horizontally. Put one layer into the prepared tin, cut side up, and brush with half the coffee and liqueur mixture. Set aside while making the mousse.
4. In a small pan, soak the gelatine in 2 tablespoons of the water with the lemon juice for 5 minutes until spongy.
5. Melt the granulated sugar in another pan with 3 tablespoons water and boil until it turns to a brown caramel. Pour in 5 tablespoons of water very carefully – it will hiss alarmingly. Cook over a low heat until the caramel has dissolved. Cool slightly.
6. Whisk the eggs and caster sugar in a heatproof bowl set over (not in) a pan of simmering water until mousse-like and thick. Remove from the heat and whisk for a further 2 minutes, until cool.
7. Dissolve the soaked gelatine very gently without boiling until clear. Do not stir. Stir into the mousse with the caramel mixture. Stir gently over a bowl of ice until beginning to thicken and set.
8. Lightly whip the cream and fold into the mixture. Pour the mousse into the cake tin.
9. Place the other half of the cake cut side up on top of the mousse and press down gently. Brush the cake with the remaining coffee and liqueur mixture. Cover with clingfilm and chill in the refrigerator for up to 6 hours, until set.
10. To remove the cake from the tin: loosen the sides by wrapping the cake tin in a cloth dipped in very hot water. Push the mousse cake out of the tin on the loose base. Using a fish slice, ease the cake on to a serving plate.

11. Before serving, dust the top heavily with sifted cocoa powder and decorate with the chocolate shavings.

NOTE: The cake can be made up to the end of stage 9 up to 2 weeks in advance and frozen. Remove from the tin while still frozen and allow to defrost in the refrigerator.

Suggested dessert wine: BUAL OR MALMSEY MADEIRA

Suggested main course: Any European-style main course

CANDIED CHEESECAKE

SERVES 6

For the crust
140g/5oz digestive biscuits, crushed
30g/1oz cocoa powder, sifted
85g/3oz butter, melted and cooled

For the filling
85g/3oz raisins
675g/1½lb cream cheese, softened
1 × 400g/14oz can of sweetened condensed milk
3 eggs, beaten
85g/3oz orange chopped mixed peel
15g/½oz plain flour
grated zest of 1 orange

To decorate
icing sugar

To serve
orange and caramel sauce (see page 218)

1. Preheat the oven to 150°C/300°F/gas mark 2. Line the base of a 27.5cm/11in springform tin with a disc of greaseproof paper.
2. In a bowl, mix together the crust ingredients and put the mixture into the tin, pressing down evenly and firmly over the base. Chill in the refrigerator while making the filling.
3. Place the raisins in a small bowl and cover with hot water. Leave to soak for 15 minutes, then drain and discard the soaking water.
4. In a large bowl, beat the cream cheese until fluffy. Gradually add the condensed milk, beating until smooth. Add the eggs gradually and mix well.
5. In a small bowl, toss the mixed peel with the raisins, flour and orange zest. Stir the fruit into the cream cheese mixture. Pour on top of the crust base.
6. Bake in the centre of the oven for 1½ hours. Switch off the oven and leave the cheesecake inside with the door closed for another hour. (As the heat slowly decreases it will continue to cook the cheesecake very gently.)
7. Remove the cheesecake from the oven and allow to cool completely to room temperature before refrigerating (if it is refrigerated while still warm the surface will crack).
8. To unmould: loosen the sides with a knife and gently remove the springform tin ring. Slide the cheesecake on to a serving plate and chill in the refrigerator.
9. Just before serving, dust heavily with sifted icing sugar. Serve well chilled with orange and caramel sauce.

Suggested dessert wine: AUSTRALIAN OR CALIFORNIAN ORANGE MUSCAT

Suggested main course: A simple poultry or fish dish is ideal as this is quite a rich dessert

CUSTARDS AND CREAMS

BREAD AND BUTTER PUDDING

This classic English favourite can be given a Continental touch made with slices of brioche or panettone.

SERVES 4

2 slices of white bread
30g/1oz butter
2 tablespoons currants and sultanas, mixed
2 teaspoons chopped mixed peel
2 eggs
1 egg yolk
1 rounded tablespoon sugar
290ml/½ pint creamy milk
vanilla essence
ground cinnamon
demerara sugar

1. Spread the bread with the butter. Cut into quarters. Arrange in a shallow ovenproof dish, buttered side up, and sprinkle with the currants, sultanas and peel.
2. Make the custard: mix the eggs and egg yolk with the sugar and stir in the milk and vanilla.
3. Strain the custard carefully over the bread and leave to soak for 30 minutes. Sprinkle with cinnamon and demerara sugar.
4. Preheat the oven to 180°C/350°F/gas mark 4.
5. Place the pudding in a roasting pan half-filled with hot water (a bain-marie) and cook in the centre of the oven for about 45 minutes, or until the custard is set and the top is brown and crusty.

NOTE: The pudding may be baked quite successfully without the bain-marie, but if used it will ensure a smooth, not bubbly custard.

Suggested dessert wine: SAUTERNES/ BARSAC

Suggested main course: Winter casserole

CRÈME CARAMEL

SERVES 4–5

110g/4oz granulated sugar
4 tablespoons water
4 eggs
2 tablespoons caster sugar
570ml/1 pint water
vanilla essence

1. Preheat the oven to 150°C/300°F/gas mark 2. Warm a soufflé or other ovenproof dish in it.
2. Place the granulated sugar in a heavy saucepan and allow it to melt slowly. Once it has melted, boil rapidly until it turns a good toffee brown. Pour into the hot soufflé dish and coat all over by carefully tipping the dish. Leave until cold.
3. Beat the eggs and caster sugar together with a wooden spoon.
4. Scald the milk by bringing it to just below boiling point and stir it into the egg mixture. Add the vanilla essence. Strain into the prepared dish. Cover with kitchen foil.
5. Stand the dish in a roasting pan half-filled with hot water (a bain-marie) and cook in the preheated oven for 1 hour, or until the custard has set.
6. Allow to cool until tepid or stone-cold, then turn out on to a dish with a good lip.

NOTE: The caramel can be made in a microwave. Put the sugar and water into a shallow dish. Cover with clingfilm and pierce. Microwave on HIGH for 2 minutes. Stir, then microwave for a further 6 minutes. Swirl it carefully around the dish.

Suggested dessert wine: BUAL/ MALMSEY MADEIRA

Suggested main course: Braised chicken or rabbit

CREAMY PRUNE CUSTARDS

Like most custards, this is best made the day before and served chilled.

SERVES 6

110g/4oz no-need-to-soak prunes, stoned and roughly chopped
3 tablespoons Armagnac
290ml/½ pint milk
340ml/12fl oz single cream
30g/1oz caster sugar
½ teaspoon vanilla essence
4 egg yolks
1 egg

To serve
150ml/¼ pint double cream, lightly whipped
cocoa powder
hazelnut and coffee biscuits (see page 235)

1. Preheat the oven to 140°C/275°F/gas mark 1. Mix the prunes with the Armagnac and set aside.
2. Place the milk, cream and sugar in a saucepan and scald by bringing to just below boiling point. Add the vanilla.
3. In a bowl, beat the egg yolks with the whole egg with a wooden spoon. Pour over the scalded milk and mix thoroughly. Strain the mixture into another bowl and add the prunes with the Armagnac.
4. Pour the mixture into 6 × 150ml/¼ pint ramekin dishes, making sure the prunes are evenly distributed between them. Place the ramekins in a roasting pan and pour in hot water to come halfway up the sides (a bain-marie).
5. Bake in the centre of the oven for 35–40 minutes, or until the custards are just set. Lift out the ramekins from the water and allow to cool. Refrigerate overnight.
6. Before serving, top each ramekin with a good dollop of whipped cream, dust lightly with sifted cocoa powder and serve with hazelnut and coffee biscuits.

Suggested dessert wine: VIN SANTO

Suggested main course: A spicy dish, after which this dessert will help soothe the palate

TROPICAL FLOATING ISLANDS

An old-fashioned dessert that tastes as good as in our childhood memories of it. This revised recipe has a tropical twist.

SERVES 8

oil for greasing

For the meringue
6 egg whites (save the yolks for the crème anglaise)
a pinch of salt
85g/3oz caster sugar
85g/3oz icing sugar

To serve
1 quantity passionfruit crème anglaise (see page 226)
1 quantity praline (see page 187)

1. Preheat the oven to 180°C/350°F/gas mark 4. Oil 8 × 150ml/¼ pint ramekin dishes and line the bases with discs of greased greaseproof paper.
2. Make the meringue: whisk the egg whites with the salt until stiff.
3. Sift the caster and icing sugars together. Add a tablespoon at a time to the egg whites, whisking until very stiff and shiny. Spoon the meringue mixture into the prepared ramekin dishes, smoothing the tops. Place the ramekins in a deep roasting pan and pour in enough hot water to reach two-thirds of the way up the sides of the ramekins (a bain-marie).
4. Bake in the centre of the oven for 30 minutes, or until the meringue feels firm to the touch. Remove the ramekins from the bain-marie and leave to cool. Run a sharp knife around the sides of the ramekins and turn out the meringues on to a plate. Refrigerate.
5. Chill the passionfruit crème anglaise well. Crush the praline.
6. To serve: place a meringue in a deep dessert plate. Pour a very generous amount of crème anglaise around it. Scatter the praline crumbs on top of the meringue and sprinkle some over the crème anglaise. Serve immediately.

Suggested dessert wine: MOSCATO D'ASTI/MUSCAT DE BEAUMES-DE-VENISE

Suggested main course: A traditional roast beef meal

CRÈME BRÛLÉE

Crème brûlée has ancient origins. In England it dates back to the eighteenth century when it was called 'burnt cream' and was a speciality of Trinity College, Cambridge. Crème brûlée is best started a day in advance.

SERVES 4

290ml/½ pint double cream
1 vanilla pod or 1 teaspoon vanilla essence
4 egg yolks
1 tablespoon caster sugar

For the topping
caster sugar

1. Put the cream with the vanilla pod, if using, into a saucepan and scald by bringing to just below boiling point, making sure it does not boil. Remove the vanilla pod.
2. Preheat the oven to 170°C/325°F/gas mark 3.
3. Beat the egg yolks with the sugar and when light and fluffy, stir in the warm cream. Place the mixture in the top of a double saucepan, or in a heatproof bowl set over (not in) a saucepan of simmering water, over a low heat. Stir continuously with a wooden spoon until the custard is thick enough to coat the back of the spoon. If using vanilla essence, add it now.
4. Pour the custard into an ovenproof serving dish, place in a roasting pan half-filled with hot water (a bain-marie) and bake in the preheated oven for 12 minutes to create a good skin on top. Remove and cool, then cover with clingfilm and refrigerate overnight. On no account break the top skin.
5. Next day preheat the grill to its highest setting.
6. Sprinkle the top of the custard with a 5mm/¼in even layer of caster sugar. To do this, stand the dish on a tray or large sheet of greaseproof paper and sift the sugar over the dish and the tray or paper. In this way you will get an even layer of sugar. Collect the sugar falling wide for re-use.
7. Put the custard under the very hot grill, as close as you can get it to the heat. The sugar will melt and caramelize before the custard underneath it boils. Watch carefully, turning the custard if the sugar is browning unevenly.
8. Allow to cool completely before serving. The top should be hard and crackly.
9. To serve: crack the top with the serving spoon and give each diner some custard (which should be creamy and just set) and a piece of caramel. Crème brûlée is also good made in individual ramekins. In this case, bake the custard for only 5 minutes.

NOTE: If making crème brûlée for more than 4 or 5 people, either make in individual ramekin dishes or in more than one large dish.

Suggested dessert wine: BUAL/ MALMSEY MADEIRA

Suggested main course: Any main course

MANGO AND COCONUT BURNT CUSTARD

This is a tropical version of crème brûlée using coconut milk and fresh mangoes. Like classic crème brûlée, it is best made the day before.

SERVES 6

250ml/8fl oz double cream
250ml/8fl oz thick coconut milk
55g/2oz desiccated coconut
55g/2oz caster sugar
6 egg yolks
1 large ripe mango, peeled and cut into small dice
1 tablespoon white rum (optional)
4 teaspoons soft light brown sugar

1. Bring the cream, coconut milk and desiccated coconut to the boil in a large heavy saucepan. Remove from the heat, cover and set aside for 30 minutes to infuse.
2. Preheat the oven to 180°C/350°F/gas mark 4.
3. In a large bowl, mix the caster sugar with the egg yolks and strain the infused cream mixture on top. Mix thoroughly. Discard the coconut pulp.
4. In a small bowl, mix the mango dice with the rum. Distribute the mango among 6 × 150ml/¼ pint capacity ramekin dishes or a large shallow gratin dish, and pour the cream on top.
5. Place the ramekins or gratin dish in a deep baking dish and pour in hot water to come halfway up the sides (a bain-marie). Bake in the centre of the oven until the custards are just set, about 45 minutes for small ones, 1 hour for large.
6. Remove the custards from the oven and allow to cool completely, then cover with clingfilm and refrigerate, ideally overnight.
7. Preheat the grill to its highest setting.
8. Sprinkle the top of each custard with an even layer of brown sugar and put them on a baking tray.
9. When the grill is blazing hot, put the custards under it as close as possible to the heat. The sugar will melt and caramelize before the custard underneath it boils. Watch carefully, turning the custard if the sugar is browning unevenly.
10. Allow to cool completely before using. The top should be hard and crisp.

Suggested dessert wine: MUSCAT DE BEAUMES-DE-VENISE/MOSCATEL DE VALENCIA

Suggested main course: Thai, Indian or Mexican-style meal

COEURS À LA CRÈME WITH STRAWBERRIES IN PORT

This is a classic French dessert and best started 4 days in advance.

SERVES 4

225g/8oz cottage cheese, drained
55g/2oz icing sugar
290ml/½ pint double cream
2 egg whites

To serve
strawberries in port (see page 123)

To decorate
sprigs of fresh mint

1. On the first day: push the cheese through a sieve into a bowl. Stir the icing sugar and cream into it and mix thoroughly.
2. Whisk the egg whites until stiff. Fold into the cheese mixture.
3. Line 4 heart-shaped coeurs à la crème moulds with clean muslin and spoon in the cheese mixture. Place in a deep dish and leave to drain in a cool place for 3–4 days.
4. To serve: turn out the coeurs à la crème on to individual serving dishes, carefully peeling off the muslin. Spoon the strawberries and sauce around. Decorate each with a sprig of mint.

NOTE: Classically, coeurs à la crème are made in small heart-shaped ceramic moulds with drainage holes (hence the name). If you do not have heart-shaped moulds, individual sweet cheeses can be made by filling small ramekin dishes with the cheese mixture, covering with muslin secured with rubber bands, and then inverting the ramekins on to a wire rack to drain.

Suggested dessert wine: OLD TAWNY PORT, LIGHTLY CHILLED

Suggested main course: A summer barbecue, roast lamb or chicken

GRAPE AND MASCARPONE CREAM

Originally from Lombardy in Italy, Mascarpone cheese has become very popular in this country, mainly due to its rich and creamy texture – it tastes more like cream than cheese. The Italians eat Mascarpone plain with sugar, flavoured with coffee or *eau-de-vie*, and with summer fruits.

SERVES 6

140g/5oz white seedless grapes
140g/5oz black seedless grapes
2 tablespoons sweet white wine
2 eggs, separated
255g/9oz Mascarpone cheese
110g/4oz caster sugar
a few drops of vanilla essence
110ml/4fl oz double cream
85g/3oz amaretti biscuits

To decorate
cocoa powder

1. Soak the grapes in the wine and set aside.
2. Beat the egg yolks with the Mascarpone and all but 1 tablespoon of the sugar. Add the vanilla.
3. Lightly whip the cream and gently fold into the Mascarpone mixture.
4. Whisk the egg whites until stiff, then add the remaining sugar, whisking until shiny and thick. Fold into the cream and Mascarpone mixture and gently mix in the grapes with the soaking wine.
5. Put the amaretti biscuits into a plastic bag and crush with a rolling pin or the bottom of a heavy saucepan.
6. Layer the mixture up: start with a thin layer of crushed biscuits and spoon over one-third of the mixture. Continue layering, finishing with a layer of cream. Chill well in the refrigerator for up to 4 hours.
7. Just before serving, dust lightly with sifted cocoa powder.

NOTE: This cream is best made on the day that it is to be served.

Suggested dessert wine: VOUVRAY MOELLEUX/COTEAUYX DU LAYON

Suggested main course: Roast lamb or pork

VANILLA AND STRAWBERRY BAVAROIS

A very delicate recipe that looks as good as it tastes. A refreshing change from ice cream.

SERVES 6

2 vanilla pods, split in half lengthwise
290ml/½ pint milk
6 eggs, separated
55g/2oz caster sugar
3 tablespoons water
20g/¾oz powdered gelatine
200ml/7oz double cream, lightly whipped
oil for greasing
450g/1lb strawberries, hulled

To serve
strawberry sauce (see page 210)

1. Put the vanilla pods into a saucepan with the milk and scald by bringing to just below boiling point.
2. Whisk the egg yolks and sugar together in a heatproof bowl set over (not in) a saucepan of simmering water and keep whisking until very thick.
3. Remove the vanilla pod from the milk and scrap the seeds back into the milk. Stir the milk into the yolk and sugar mixture. Return to the saucepan and reheat, stirring continuously with a wooden spoon until the custard is thick enough to coat the back of the spoon. Do not boil or the custard will curdle.
4. Put the water into a small saucepan and sprinkle on the gelatine. Leave for 5 minutes until spongy.
5. Dissolve the gelatine over a low heat without boiling until clear. Do not stir. Pour half the warm liquid gelatine into the custard mixture. Pour the mixture into a large bowl and stir occasionally until on the point of setting. Fold in the cream.
6. Turn half the mixture into 6 lightly oiled 150ml/¼ pint ramekin dishes and chill in the refrigerator while making the strawberry bavarois.
7. Save 6 strawberries to decorate. Liquidize or mash the remaining strawberries to a pulp. Reheat the remaining gelatine and gently fold it into the other half of the vanilla bavarois together with the strawberry puree. Spoon the mixture on top of the vanilla bavarois and smooth the top with a spoon. Cover and leave to set in the refrigerator for at least 6 hours.
8. To serve: flood the bases of 6 dessert plates with the strawberry sauce. Turn the bavarois out carefully, using a knife to loosen it, or dip the ramekins very quickly in boiling water. Decorate each bavarois with a strawberry and serve.

NOTE: Bavarois should not be made more than a day in advance.

Suggested dessert wine: SAUTERNES/ BARSAC

Suggested main course: This is rich but delicate enough to be served after most main courses

TRIFLE

SERVES 6

1 Victoria sandwich cake, preferably stale
very good-quality raspberry jam
4 tablespoons sherry
2 tablespoons brandy
290ml/½ pint milk
5 egg yolks
2 tablespoons caster sugar
2 drops of vanilla essence
290ml/½ pint double cream
30g/1oz split blanched almonds, toasted
a few ratafia biscuits (optional)

1. Cut the sponge cake into thick pieces. Sandwich the pieces together sparingly with jam. Pile them into a large glass serving dish.
2. Pour over the sherry and brandy and leave to soak while you prepare the custard.
3. Put the milk into a saucepan and scald by bringing to just below boiling point.
4. In a large bowl, lightly beat the yolks and sugar with a wooden spoon. Pour the scalding milk on to them, stirring.
5. Return the mixture to the pan and reheat carefully, stirring all the time, until the mixture is thick enough to coat the back of the spoon. Care must be taken not to boil the custard, or it will curdle. Add the vanilla essence.
6. Strain on to the cake and leave to get completely cold.
7. Whip the cream until fairly stiff and spread or pipe over the trifle.
8. Decorate with the almonds and the ratafia biscuits, if using.

Suggested dessert wine: SWEET OLOROSO SHERRY

Suggested main course: Chicken or guinea-fowl

TIRAMISÙ

SERVES 8

6 egg yolks
scant 150ml/¼ pint Marsala
5 tablespoons dry white wine
85g/3oz icing sugar, or more to taste
500g/1lb 2oz Mascarpone or cream cheese
10 amaretti biscuits
24 boudoir biscuits (sponge fingers)
5 tablespoons strong black coffee
unsweetened cocoa powder, for sprinkling

1. Mix the egg yolks, half the Marsala, the white wine, icing sugar and Mascarpone together to make a cream, but if making this for children or teetotallers leave out the Marsala and white wine.
2. Dip the biscuits in the remaining Marsala mixed with the coffee (once again, leave out the Marsala if so desired), taking care not to make the biscuits so soggy that they break. Line a dish about 25cm/10in square with a layer of biscuits and a layer of the cream.
3. Repeat, until all the ingredients have been used, ending with a layer of cream. Sprinkle a thin layer of unsweetened cocoa powder on top and refrigerate for a few hours before serving.

Suggested dessert wine: VIN SANTO/ TAWNY PORT

Suggested main course: Almost any dish

SOUFFLÉS AND MOUSSES

HOT CHOCOLATE SOUFFLÉ

To make a successful chocolate soufflé you must have everything organized before you start to cook and work as quickly as possible. Hot soufflés require careful preparation and timing but are very well worth the effort.

SERVES 4

melted butter
55g/2oz caster sugar, plus 1 teaspoon for the dish
110g/4oz plain chocolate
4 egg yolks
5 egg whites
icing sugar

1. Preheat the oven to 200°C/400°F/gas mark 6. Preheat a baking sheet. Prepare the soufflé dish by brushing the inside with melted butter and dusting it with 1 teaspoon caster sugar.
2. Chop the chocolate with a large knife and put it into a heatproof bowl set over (not in) a saucepan of simmering water, stirring until the chocolate has completely melted. Remove from the heat.
3. Beat the remaining sugar and the egg yolks together for 1 minute with a wooden spoon until thick and fluffy. Add the egg-yolk mixture to the chocolate, mixing well – it will thicken slightly.
4. Whisk the whites until they will stand in soft peaks when the whisk is withdrawn from the bowl. Whisk in 1 teaspoon caster sugar, until stiff and shiny. Gently but thoroughly fold into the chocolate mixture.
5. Turn into the soufflé dish but do not fill more than two-thirds of the dish. Run the end of a wooden spoon handle around the edge of the soufflé mixture. This gives a 'top hat' appearance to the cooked soufflé.
6. Bake in the preheated oven on the hot baking sheet for 20–25 minutes. Test by giving the dish a slight shake or push. If the soufflé wobbles alarmingly, it needs further cooking; if it wobbles slightly, it is ready. Dust lightly with icing sugar and serve immediately.

Suggested dessert wine: AUSTRALIAN LIQUEUR MUSCAT/YOUNG LBV PORT

Suggested main course: Roast beef or lamb

PINEAPPLE AND COCONUT SOUFFLÉ

SERVES 4

melted butter
30g/1oz caster sugar
1 × 425g/15oz can of pineapple in syrup
2 tablespoons white rum (optional)
45g/1½oz unsalted butter
45g/1½oz plain flour
grated zest of ½ lemon
150ml/¼ pint thick coconut milk
4 egg whites

To decorate
icing sugar

1. Preheat the oven to 200°C/400°F/gas mark 6. Place a baking sheet on the middle shelf to heat. Brush a 1.2 litre/2 pint soufflé dish inside with melted butter and dust with 1 teaspoon of the caster sugar.
1. Drain the pineapple and reserve 100ml/3fl oz of the syrup. Cut the pineapple into very small dice. Add the rum, if using, and reserve.
3. Melt the butter in a medium saucepan and add the flour. Cook for 1 minute, then remove from the heat. Add the lemon zest, coconut milk and reserved pineapple syrup. Return the pan to the heat and bring very gently to the boil, stirring continuously. Simmer for 2 minutes. Transfer the mixture to a large bowl and allow to cool.
4. Whisk the egg whites until they stand in soft peaks when the whisk is withdrawn from the bowl. Whisk in the remaining caster sugar until stiff and shiny. Using a large metal spoon, fold gently but thoroughly into the custard mixture.
5. Pour half the mixture into the prepared soufflé dish and gently spoon all but 3 tablespoons of the diced pineapple on top. Pour the remaining soufflé mixture on top – do not fill more than two-thirds of the dish. Run the handle of a wooden spoon around the top of the soufflé mixture. This gives a 'top hat' appearance to the cooked soufflé.
6. Bake on the hot baking sheet for 20 minutes. Test by giving the dish a slight shake and push. If it wobbles alarmingly, it needs further cooking; if it wobbles slightly it is ready. Remove from the oven, dust with sifted icing sugar, decorate with the reserved diced pineapple and serve immediately.

NOTES: When making a soufflé, always remove the oven shelf above the soufflé dish, just in case the soufflé rises particularly well.

The soufflé can be prepared up to the end of stage 5 and frozen in individual soufflé dishes, then cooked from frozen for about 20 minutes.

Suggested dessert wine: MOSCATO D'ASTI

Suggested main course: Game or beef

MIXED BERRY AND MERINGUE POTS WITH RASPBERRY SAUCE

This is a luscious yet delicate dessert. After the first layer of warm meringue the coolness of the fromage frais and berries is a wonderful surprise.

SERVES 6

450g/1lb mixed fresh or frozen berries (blackcurrants, raspberries, redcurrants, blueberries, blackberries)
melted butter for greasing
juice of ½ lemon
400g/14oz fromage frais
3 teaspoons icing sugar
4 drops of vanilla essence

For the meringue
3 egg whites
170g/6oz icing sugar, sifted

To serve
raspberry sauce (see page 210)

1. Wash and drain the berries thoroughly. If using frozen berries, let them defrost. Brush 6 ramekin dishes with melted butter.
2. Put the berries and lemon juice into the ramekins.
3. In a large bowl, mix together the fromage frais, icing sugar and vanilla. Spoon the mixture over the berries, covering them completely, and place the ramekins in the freezer while making the meringue.
4. Preheat the oven to 230°C/450°F/gas mark 8.
5. Make the meringue: put the egg whites with the icing sugar into a large heatproof bowl and set over (not in) a saucepan of simmering water. Whisk with a large hand balloon whisk or electric hand whisk, until the meringue is thick and will hold its shape. This may well take up to 10 minutes of vigorous beating. Remove the bowl from the heat and whisk for a further 2 minutes.
6. Remove the ramekins from the freezer. The crème fraiche should be very cold but not frozen. Spoon the meringue on top, forming peaks.
7. Place the ramekins on a baking sheet. Bake in the top of the oven for 3–5 minutes, until the meringue has browned. Remove from the oven, drizzle with the raspberry sauce, and serve immediately. Hand the remaining sauce separately.

NOTE: This recipe looks spectacular if made in individual ramekin dishes with the meringue piled high. It can also be made in a 1.2 litre/2 pint soufflé dish.

Suggested dessert wine: MOSCATO D'ASTI/DEMI-SEC CHAMPAGNE

Suggested main course: Any meat, fish, poultry or game dish

COLD LEMON SOUFFLÉ

SERVES 4

grated zest and juice of 2 large lemons
7g/¼oz powdered gelatine
3 eggs, separated
140g/5oz caster sugar
150ml/¼ pint double cream, lightly whipped
icing sugar (optional)

To decorate
150ml/¼ pint double cream, whipped
wafer-thin lemon slices
nibbed almonds, toasted

1. Put the lemon juice into a small saucepan, sprinkle over the gelatine and leave for 5 minutes until spongy.
2. Place the egg yolks, sugar and lemon zest in a mixing bowl and whisk together with an electric beater (or with a balloon whisk or rotary beater with the bowl set over a saucepan of simmering water). Whisk until very thick. If whisking by hand over hot water, remove from heat and whisk for a few minutes longer, until the mixture is lukewarm.
3. Dissolve the gelatine over a low heat without boiling until liquid and clear, then add to the mousse mixture. Stir gently until the mixture is on the point of setting, then fold in the cream. Taste and if too tart, sift in a little icing sugar; if too bland, add a little more lemon juice.
4. Whisk the egg whites until stiff but not dry and fold them into the soufflé with a large metal spoon.
5. Pour the mixture into a soufflé dish and leave to set in the refrigerator for 2–3 hours. Decorate with rosettes of cream, lemon slices and almonds.

NOTE: This dish can be given a more soufflé-like appearance by tying a double band of oiled paper round the top of the dish so that it projects about 2.5cm/1in above the rim, before pouring in the mixture. (The dish must be of a size that would not quite contain the mixture without the added depth given by the paper band.) Pour in the soufflé mixture to come about 2.5cm/1in up the paper, above the rim of the dish. When the soufflé is set, carefully remove the paper and press the almonds round the exposed sides.

Suggested dessert wine: VOUVRAY/COTEAUX DU LAYON/MOSCATO D'ASTI

Suggested main course: Vegetarian or chicken risotto

CHOCOLATE MOUSSE

A favourite with adults and children alike, this mousse should be made with the finest chocolate available.

SERVES 4

110g/4oz plain chocolate
4 eggs, separated

1. Chop the chocolate into even-sized pieces. Put into a heatproof bowl set over (not in) a saucepan of simmering water. Allow it to melt.
2. Stir the melted chocolate into the egg yolks. Mix well. Whisk the egg whites until quite stiff. Fold the whites into the chocolate mixture.
3. Turn immediately into a soufflé dish or individual pots or glasses.
4. Chill until set, preferably overnight, but for at least 4 hours.

Suggested dessert wine: AUSTRALIAN LIQUEUR MUSCAT

Suggested main course: Roast chicken or light meat dish

CHOCOLATE MOUSSE WITH COINTREAU ORANGES

This is an intensely rich chocolate mousse recipe, not for the faint-hearted!

SERVES 6

3 oranges
1½ tablespoons Cointreau
70g/2½oz granulated sugar
110ml/4fl oz water
3 egg yolks
170g/6oz good-quality dark chocolate, chopped
340ml/12fl oz double cream

1. Grate the zest of 2 oranges. Using a sharp knife, peel all 3 oranges as you would an apple, removing all pith. Working over a bowl to collect the juices, cut out the orange segments, leaving behind the membranes. Mix together the orange segments, juice and Cointreau and chill in the refrigerator while making the mousse.
2. Put the sugar and water into a small saucepan and heat gently until the sugar has dissolved completely, then bring to the boil. Boil to the thread stage (see page 42).
3. Put the egg yolks into a large bowl, whisk lightly and pour on the warm sugar syrup (do not allow the syrup to touch the beaters if doing this in a machine or it will harden). Continue whisking until the mixture is thick and mousse-like.
4. Melt the chocolate carefully in a heatproof bowl fitted over (not in) a saucepan of simmering water. Using a large metal spoon, fold the chocolate and orange zest into the egg mixture. Lightly whip the cream and immediately fold into the mixture.
5. Divide the orange segments and liquid among 6 tall glasses, or place in a glass bowl, and spoon the mousse on top. Chill in the refrigerator for at least 4 hours.

NOTE: This mousse can be made a day in advance. Remove from the refrigerator 10 minutes before serving.

Suggested dessert wine: AUSTRALIAN LIQUEUR MUSCAT

Suggested main course: Any dish that is not too rich or spicy. Avoid curries

MERINGUE DESSERTS

MERINGUES (SWISS MERINGUES)

A Swiss pastry chef called Gasparini is credited with the creation of meringues. The great nineteenth-century chef Carême introduced piped meringues: previously they were shaped with spoons.

MAKES 50 MINIATURE OR 12 LARGE MERINGUES

4 egg whites
a pinch of salt
225g/8oz caster sugar

For the filling
double cream, whipped

1. Preheat the oven to 110°C/225°F/gas mark ½.
2. Line 2 baking sheets with silicone baking paper.
3. Whisk the egg whites with the salt until stiff but not dry.
4. Add 2 tablespoons of the sugar and whisk again until very stiff and shiny.
5. Fold in the remaining sugar.
6. Drop the meringue mixture on to the lined baking sheets in spoonfuls set fairly far apart. Use a teaspoon for tiny meringues; a dessertspoon for larger ones.
7. Bake in the preheated oven for about 2 hours until the meringues are dry right through and will lift easily off the paper.
8. When cold, sandwich the meringues together in pairs with whipped cream.

Suggested dessert wine: MOSCATO D'ASTI

Suggested main course: Mayonnaise-based dish or cold meats

MERINGUE BASKETS

SERVES 6

2 egg whites
a pinch of salt
110g/4oz caster sugar

For the filling
double cream, lightly whipped
strawberries or raspberries

1. Preheat the oven to 110°C/225°F/gas mark ½. Line 2 baking sheets with silicone baking paper.
2. Whisk the egg whites with the salt to a stiff snow. Whisk in 2 tablespoons of the sugar and continue to whisk until the mixture is stiff and shiny. Fold in the remaining sugar with a large metal spoon.
3. Put the mixture into a piping bag fitted with a rose nozzle and pipe on to the lined baking sheets to form little baskets.
4. Place in the preheated oven to dry out for 2 hours. Remove from the oven, carefully peel off the lining paper and allow to cool on a wire rack.
5. Place a little cream in each basket and fill with strawberries or raspberries.

Suggested dessert wine: MOSCATO D'ASTI

Suggested main course: Mayonnaise-based dish or cold meats

CINNAMON MERINGUE NESTS WITH PERSIMMON CREAM AND RED WINE SAUCE

Persimmons are sometimes called kaquis and look like plum tomatoes. They have a deliciously sweet and soft pulp and taste best when very ripe.

SERVES 6

For the meringue nests
1 quantity Swiss meringue (see page 171)
1 teaspoon ground cinnamon

For the cream
3 very ripe persimmons
2 teaspoons icing sugar, sifted
3 tablespoons lemon juice
190ml/⅓ pint double cream

To decorate
4 fresh mint leaves

To serve
red wine syrup sauce (see page 222)

1. Preheat the oven to 110°C/225°F/gas mark ½.
2. Make the meringue and mix in the ground cinnamon. Pipe into 6 nests and bake as described in the meringue recipe. Allow to cool completely before assembling the dish.

2. Make the cream: halve the persimmons and scoop out the pulp with a spoon. Push the pulp through a sieve into a small saucepan together with the icing sugar and lemon juice.
3. Bring to the boil, reduce the heat and simmer for about 10 minutes, until the pulp is reduced by half. Transfer to a bowl to cool completely.
4. Lightly whip the cream. Fold the cooled persimmon purée gently into the cream. Chill in the refrigerator until ready to assemble the dish.
5. To serve: spoon or pipe a generous amount of the cream into each meringue nest, place on a dessert plate and decorate with a mint leaf. Drizzle some of the red wine syrup sauce on top and hand the remaining sauce separately. Serve immediately.

NOTE: The meringue nests can be made up to 3 days in advance and stored in an airtight container.

Suggested dessert wine: AUSTRALIAN LIQUEUR MUSCAT

Suggested main course: Almost any type of main course

COCONUT MERINGUES WITH GUAVA AND HONEY SAUCE

SERVES 6

For the meringue
1 quantity Swiss meringue (see page 171)
55g/2oz desiccated coconut

For the sauce
2 ripe pink guavas, peeled, halved and chopped
150ml/¼ pint medium-sweet red wine
110ml/4fl oz water
3 tablespoons lemon juice
3 tablespoons clear honey
½ teaspoon ground cinnamon

For the filling
190ml/⅓ pint double cream

To decorate
4 fresh mint leaves

1. Preheat the oven to 110°C/225°F/gas mark ½.
2. Make the meringue and fold the coconut into the mixture. Drop tablespoons of the mixture on to a baking sheet lined with silicone baking paper and bake until dry, as described in the meringue recipe. Cool completely before assembling.
3. Make the sauce: mix all the ingredients in a small saucepan and cook over a low heat for about 15 minutes, or until the guavas are very soft. Pour the mixture into a blender and process to a smooth sauce the consistency of double cream. If too thick, add a few tablespoons of water. Pass through a fine sieve, taste and add more lemon juice if too sweet, more honey if too tart. Chill in the refrigerator.
4. Lightly whip the cream and use to sandwich the meringues together in pairs.
5. To serve: spoon the guava sauce on to each dessert plate and place 2–3 sandwiched meringues on top. Decorate with a mint leaf and serve immediately.

Suggested dessert wine: AUSTRALIAN OR CALIFORNIAN ORANGE MUSCAT

Suggested main course: A spicy meat or vegetarian dish

HAZELNUT, CHOCOLATE AND BLACKBERRY MERINGUE CAKE

This meringue cake looks spectacular and can be prepared a day ahead and assembled shortly before serving. It is a must for all meringue lovers!

SERVES 6

For the meringue cakes
oil for greasing
6 egg whites
a pinch of salt
1 teaspoon cream of tartar
140g/5oz caster sugar
140g/5oz hazelnuts, ground or finely chopped
140g/5oz dark chocolate, coarsely grated

For the filling
150ml/¼ pint double cream, lightly whipped
255g/9oz blackberries
1 teaspoon icing sugar
1 tablespoon crème de Cassis

To decorate
55g/2oz dark chocolate, melted

To serve
a few extra blackberries

1. Preheat the oven to 190°C/375°F/gas mark 5. Line two 20cm/8in moule-à-manqué tins with kitchen foil and brush the foil lightly with oil.
2. Whisk the egg whites with the salt and cream of tartar until stiff, then add half the sugar and whisk until shiny and thick. Fold in the remaining sugar.
3. Mix together the nuts and chocolate. Using a large metal spoon, gently fold the nuts and chocolate into the meringue mixture. Divide the mixture between the two prepared tins.
4. Bake in the centre of the oven for about 20 minutes, then turn down oven temperature to 170°C/325°F/gas mark 3 and bake for a further 10 minutes. Remove the meringue cakes from the tins together with the foil and allow to cool on a wire rack.
5. To assemble the cake: gently peel off the foil and place the meringue cakes on a board. Mix the cream with the blackberries, icing sugar and crème de Cassis. Spread the cream over one cake and place the second one on top, with the most attractive crust uppermost, and press down gently.
6. Pour the melted chocolate into a small piping bag and slowly draw lines over the top of the cake from one side to the other. Transfer to a serving plate.
7. Serve with fresh blackberries.

NOTE: Raspberries, blueberries, loganberries or a mixture of summer berries can be substituted for the blackberries.

Suggested dessert wine: AUSTRALIAN LIQUEUR MUSCAT

Suggested main course: Most main courses and summer barbecues

MERINGUE ROULADE WITH TUTTI FRUTTI CREAM AND STRAWBERRY SAUCE

The idea for this superb recipe came from Lee Francis, a teacher at Leith's.

SERVES 6

For the roulade
4 egg whites
a pinch of salt
225g/8oz caster sugar
1 teaspoon cornflour
1 teaspoon vanilla essence
1 teaspoon vinegar

For the tutti frutti cream
150ml/¼ pint double cream
45g/1½oz glacé cherries, roughly chopped
85g/3oz chopped mixed peel
45g/1½oz nibbed almonds, lightly toasted

To decorate
icing sugar

To serve
strawberry sauce (see page 210)

1. Take a large roasting pan and cut a double layer of silicone baking paper slightly bigger than it. Lay this in the pan (don't worry if the edges stick up untidily round the sides). Preheat the oven to 200°C/400°F/gas mark 6.
2. Whisk the egg whites with the salt until stiff. Gradually add the sugar, whisking until you can stand a spoon in the mixture.
3. Add the cornflour, vanilla and vinegar. Spread the mixture evenly on the paper in the roasting pan. Bake for 15 minutes, or until the meringue top is pale biscuit colour and firm to the touch. Remove from the oven, slide the roulade and paper out of the roasting pan on to a wire rack and leave to cool.
4. Lightly whip the cream and gently mix in the cherries, peel and nuts.
5. Before filling: flip the roulade over on to a tea-towel. Carefully peel off the lining paper, then spread the tutti frutti cream evenly over the roulade. Roll up like a Swiss roll on to a serving dish and, just before serving, dust with a little sifted icing sugar over the top.
6. Hand the strawberry sauce separately.

Suggested dessert wine: MUSCAT DE BEAUMES-DE-VENISE/MOSCATEL DE VALENCIA

Suggested main course: A dish with mayonnaise. Meringues are particularly good after these

SORBET AND MERINGUE PIE

SERVES 6

For the meringue
4 egg whites
225g/8oz icing sugar, sifted
3 drops of vanilla essence

For the sorbets
570ml/1 pint strawberry sorbet (see page 199)
570ml/1 pint pear sorbet (see page 202)

To serve
icing sugar
strawberry sauce (see page 210)

To decorate
fresh strawberries

1. Preheat the oven to 140°C/275°F/gas mark 1. Draw 3 × 20cm/8in diameter circles on 3 pieces of silicone baking paper, turn over and use to line 3 baking sheets.
2. Put the egg whites and icing sugar into a heatproof bowl and set over (not in) a saucepan of simmering water. Using a large hand balloon whisk or electric hand whisk, whisk for up to 10 minutes, until the meringue is thick and will hold its shape.
3. Remove the bowl from the heat, add the vanilla and whisk for a further 2 minutes. Spread or pipe the mixture on to the 3 prepared circles on the silicone paper. Bake for 45–60 minutes, until dry and crisp. Cool on a wire rack.
4. Remove the sorbets from the freezer and allow to soften slightly.
5. Make the pie: line the base of a 22.5cm/9in springform tin with a disc of greaseproof paper. Place one meringue layer in the bottom. Spread over the strawberry sorbet and cover with a second layer of meringue. Spread over the pear sorbet, cover with the last meringue layer and press down gently. Cover and place in the freezer overnight.
6. Just before serving, remove the pie from the freezer and run a knife dipped in hot water around the inside of the tin to loosen the pie. Remove the sides of the tin and transfer the pie to a chopping board. Dust heavily with sifted icing sugar and cut into 6 wedges, using a sharp knife.
7. To serve: spoon some of the strawberry sauce on to a dessert plate, place a slice of pie on top, decorate with fresh strawberries and serve immediately. Hand the remaining strawberry sauce separately.

NOTES: The pie can be made up to the end of stage 5 up to 3 days in advance.
The flavour of the sorbets can be varied to taste. The pie also tastes delicious using ice creams.

Suggested dessert wine: MOSCATO D'ASTI/MUSCAT DE BEAUMES-DE-VENISE

Suggested main course: A rich main course, such as beef casserole or coq au vin, after which this dessert is very refreshing

ICE CREAMS AND SORBETS

RICH VANILLA ICE CREAM

This is the classic vanilla ice cream recipe, using real vanilla pods and enough cream to make it smooth and rich. Good with everything and at any time of day or night!

SERVES 6

70g/2½oz granulated sugar
8 tablespoons water
1 vanilla pod, split in half lengthwise
3 egg yolks
425ml/¾ pint double cream

1. Put the sugar, water and vanilla pod into a saucepan and dissolve the sugar over a low heat, stirring.
2. Beat the egg yolks well.
3. When the sugar has dissolved, bring the syrup up to boiling point and boil to the short thread stage (see page 42). Allow to cool for 1 minute. Remove the vanilla pod.
4. Whisk the egg yolks and gradually pour in the sugar syrup. Whisk until the mixture is very thick and will leave a ribbon trail.
5. Allow to cool, whisking occasionally. Fold in the cream and freeze.
6. When the ice cream is half frozen, whisk again and return to the freezer. Transfer to the refrigerator 20 minutes before serving.

Suggested dessert wine: CONSTANTIA

Suggested main course: Any main course

CINNAMON AND VANILLA ICE CREAM

The delicious combination of cinnamon and vanilla complements plums baked in red wine perfectly.

SERVES 6

1 vanilla pod, split in half lengthwise
290ml/½ pint double cream
425ml/¾ pint milk
30g/1oz caster sugar
3 cinnamon sticks, broken
½ teaspoon ground cinnamon
6 egg yolks
85g/3oz soft dark brown sugar

To serve
plums baked in red wine (see page 117)

1. In a large saucepan, mix the vanilla pod, cream, milk, caster sugar, cinnamon sticks and ground cinnamon. Bring to the boil, stirring until the sugar has dissolved completely. Remove from the heat, cover and set aside for 30 minutes to infuse.
2. Beat the egg yolks with the dark brown sugar until well combined. Gradually strain in the infused milk mixture and discard the cinnamon sticks. Pour the mixture back into the pan and cook over a low heat without boiling, stirring constantly, until the mixture thickens slightly.
3. Pour into a freezer-proof container and chill. Freeze the mixture for about 3 hours, until solid but still soft enough to give when pressed with a finger.
4. Tip the ice cream into a chilled bowl and break it up with a fork, then process or whisk until smooth, pale and creamy. Freeze again.
5. Transfer to the refrigerator 20 minutes before serving with the warm plums baked in red wine.

Suggested dessert wine: SERVE BEFORE A FORTIFIED WINE SUCH AS PORT OR BANYULS

Suggested main course: Any seafood or fish dish

Vanilla and Strawberry Bavarois

Mascarpone Ice Cream with Grilled Figs and Hazelnut and Coffee Biscuits

Frozen Rasberry Yoghurt with Chocolate Sauce

Tropical Fruit and Frozen Yoghurt Cup with Pineapple Sauce

Cinnamon Meringue Nests with Persimmon Cream and Red Wine Sauce

Hazelnut, Chocolate and Blackberry Meringue Cake

Meringue Roulade with Tutti Frutti Cream and Strawberry Sauce

Sorbet and Meringue Pie

COFFEE ICE CREAM

SERVES 4–6

4 egg yolks
85g/3oz caster sugar
a pinch of salt
425ml/¾ pint single cream
5 teaspoons instant coffee powder

1. Mix the egg yolks with the sugar and salt.
2. Place the cream and coffee in a saucepan and heat gently until the coffee dissolves.
3. Add the cream to the egg-yolk mixture, stirring all the time.
4. Pour the mixture into the top of a double saucepan or into a heatproof bowl set over (not in) a saucepan of simmering water.
5. Stir continuously until thick and creamy.
6. Strain into a bowl and allow to cool, whisking occasionally.
7. Chill, then pour into an ice tray and freeze.
8. When the ice cream is half-frozen, whisk again and return to the freezer. Transfer to the refrigerator 20 minutes before serving.

Suggested dessert wine: BUAL/ MALMSEY MADEIRA

Suggested main course: Pasta dish

COFFEE ICE CREAM CUP WITH SESAME CARAMEL SAUCE

The sesame caramel sauce can be prepared a day in advance, making this simple but elegant dessert a good choice after a more labour-intensive main course.

SERVES 6

1 quantity coffee ice cream (see page 183)

For the sesame caramel sauce
55g/2oz hazelnuts, finely chopped
2 tablespoons sesame seeds
55g/2oz caster sugar
4 tablespoons water
150ml/¼ pint double cream
2 tablespoons golden syrup
30g/1oz unsalted butter

1. Preheat the oven to 180°C/350°F/gas mark 4. Place the chopped hazelnuts and sesame seeds in a roasting pan. Toast in the oven for about 8–10 minutes, until golden-brown. Transfer to a plate to cool.
2. Make the sesame caramel sauce: put the sugar and water into a heavy saucepan and allow the sugar to melt slowly over a low heat. When the sugar has melted completely, boil rapidly until it becomes a rich brown caramel. Remove the pan from the heat and add the cream. Put the pan back on the heat and stir until the cream and caramel are well blended. Stir in the golden syrup, butter and toasted nuts and seeds. Cool before using.
3. To serve: place a tablespoon of the sauce in a tall glass and add a few tablespoons of soft coffee ice cream. Add another tablespoon of sauce and continue layering until the glass is full. Finish with a layer of sauce. Put the glasses into the freezer for at least 1 hour (they can be prepared the day before). Transfer to the refrigerator 20 minutes before serving.

NOTE: Use robust glasses that will not crack in the freezer. Sundae glasses are ideal.

Suggested dessert wine: BUAL OR MALMSEY MADEIRA

Suggested main course: Duck, fish or beef

MACAROON AND COFFEE ICE CREAM PIE

SERVES 6

For the macaroons
200g/7oz ground almonds
200g/7oz caster sugar
1 teaspoon plain flour
a few drops of vanilla essence
3 egg whites (at room temperature)

To decorate
icing sugar

To serve
1 quantity coffee ice cream (see page 183), softened
1 quantity cappuccino sauce (see page 216)

1. Preheat the oven to 180°C/350°F/gas mark 4. Line a baking sheet with silicone baking paper.
2. Make the macaroons: mix the ground almonds, sugar, flour and vanilla together in a large bowl.
3. Add the egg whites and beat very well. Spread or pipe the mixture into 3 × 18cm/7in rounds on the baking paper. Bake for 15 minutes, or until the mixture looks dry and slightly browned. Lift the baking paper from the baking sheet and turn the macaroons on to a wire rack. Peel away the paper and leave to cool.
4. To assemble: place one macaroon on a piece of greaseproof paper. Spread half the ice cream on top. Place the other macaroon layer on top and spread the remaining ice cream on top. Gently press the last macaroon layer on top. Tie a double piece of greaseproof paper around the outside and secure the ends with a paper clip or pin. Place in the freezer.
5. To serve: remove the pie from the freezer 20 minutes before serving. Remove the paper carefully, dust the top with sifted icing sugar and transfer the pie to a serving plate. Cut into 8 wedges and hand the cappuccino sauce separately.

Suggested dessert wine: BUAL OR MALMSEY MADEIRA

Suggested main course: Seafood, pasta

PRALINE AND CHIBOUST FROZEN LOAF WITH RASPBERRY SAUCE

Chiboust, a cream invented by a Parisian pastry chef in the nineteenth century, consists of equal quantities of crème pâtissière and meringue mixture. It can be used as a filling for fruit tarts and is exquisite when frozen.

SERVES 6

1 quantity praline (see page 187)

For the crème pâtissière
2 egg yolks
55g/2oz caster sugar
1 scant teaspoon plain flour
1 scant teaspoon cornflour
290ml/½ pint milk
vanilla essence
110ml/4fl oz double cream

For the meringue
3 egg whites
170g/6oz icing sugar, sifted
3 drops of vanilla essence

To serve
raspberry sauce (see page 210)

1. Make the crème pâtissière: cream the egg yolks with the sugar until pale, then mix in the flours. Pour on the milk and mix well. Place in a saucepan and bring to the boil, stirring continuously (the mixture will go alarmingly lumpy, but don't worry, keep stirring and it will become smooth). Allow to cool slightly, then add vanilla to taste. Transfer to a bowl and cover the surface with clingfilm to prevent a skin forming.
2. Make the meringue: put the egg whites and icing sugar into a mixing bowl and set over (not in) a pan of simmering water. Whisk, using a large hand balloon whisk or electric hand whisk, until the meringue is thick and will hold its shape. This may take up to 10 minutes. Add the vanilla, remove the bowl from the pan and whisk for a further 2 minutes.
3. Whip the cream lightly and fold into the crème pâtissière. Using a large metal spoon, gently fold the meringue into the crème pâtissière mixture until well incorporated.
4. Wet a 450g/1lb loaf tin and line with clingfilm overlapping the sides. Spoon half the cream and meringue mixture into the loaf tin and sprinkle with one-third of the praline. Spoon the remaining cream and meringue mixture on top and cover carefully with clingfilm. Freeze overnight.
5. To serve: remove the loaf from the freezer 20 minutes before serving and unmould on to a serving plate. Press the remaining praline over the top gently but firmly. Cut into slices, using a sharp knife, and hand the raspberry sauce separately.

NOTE: The praline can be made up a day in advance and stored in an airtight jar.

Suggested dessert wine: SAUTERNES/BARSAC

Suggested main course: Fish or poultry

PRALINE

a few drops of oil
55g/2oz unblanched almonds
55g/2oz caster sugar

1. Oil a baking sheet.
2. Put the almonds and sugar into a heavy saucepan, and set over a low heat. Stir with a metal spoon as the sugar begins to melt and brown. When thoroughly caramelized (browned), tip on to the oiled sheet.
3. Allow to cool completely, then pound to a coarse powder in a mortar or blender.
4. Store in an airtight jar.

NOTE: Whole praline almonds, as sold in the streets of Paris, are made in the same way, but are not crushed to a powder. They are sometimes used for cake decoration.

ORANGE ICE CREAM

Very easy to prepare, this recipe can also be made using any other concentrated fruit juice, with great results.

SERVES 6–8

200g/7oz frozen concentrated orange juice
170g/6oz caster sugar
3 tablespoons golden syrup
3 tablespoons lemon juice
570ml/1 pint milk
190ml/⅓ pint double cream
100ml/3fl oz single cream
grated zest and segments of 1 orange

To serve
pine nut sablés (see page 231)

1. Tip the frozen orange juice into a large bowl. When it begins to soften, add the sugar, golden syrup and lemon juice and whisk until smooth.
2. Add the milk, creams and orange zest, and whisk until the mixture is well blended and the sugar has dissolved completely. Pour the mixture into a freezer-proof container and freeze.
3. When the ice cream is half frozen, whisk again and return to the freezer.
4. Transfer the ice cream to the refrigerator 20 minutes before serving.
5. Spoon the ice cream into tall serving glasses, decorate with the orange segments and serve with the pine nut sablés.

Suggested dessert wine: AUSTRALIAN OR CALIFORNIAN ORANGE MUSCAT

Suggested main course: A spicy curry or meat stew

KUMQUAT PARFAIT WITH KUMQUAT HONEY SAUCE

SERVES 6

For the parfait
200g/7oz kumquats
225g/8oz caster sugar
190ml/⅓ pint water
thinly pared zest of 1 lemon
570ml/1 pint double cream

For the sauce
200g/7oz kumquats, thinly sliced
110ml/4fl oz sweet white wine
grated zest and juice of 1 orange
1 tablespoon clear honey

1. Make the parfait: cut the kumquats in half and remove any pips.
2. Put the sugar, water and lemon zest into a medium saucepan and heat slowly until the sugar has dissolved completely. Bring to the boil and add the halved kumquats.
3. Boil for about 10 minutes, or until the kumquats are soft. Drain the fruit and put the syrup back into the pan. Discard the lemon zest.
4. Process the kumquats to a coarse purée in a blender or food processor. (Alternatively they can be finely chopped by hand.) Reserve.
5. Bring the syrup to the boil and boil to the short thread stage (see page 42).
6. Meanwhile, whisk the egg whites to stiff peaks. If this is done in a machine, pour the bubbling syrup on to them in a steady stream while whisking, taking care not to pour the syrup on to the beaters or it will solidify. If whisking the whites by hand, and in the absence of anyone to pour while you whisk, pour the syrup on to the whites in stages, about one-third at a time, whisking hard after each addition, and working as fast as possible.
7. When all the syrup has been added, whisk hard until the mixture is stiff and shiny and absolutely stable. The meringue should not flow at all when the whisk is lifted.
8. Lightly whip the cream and fold in the kumquat purée. Gently fold the meringue into the kumquat and cream mixture.
9. Lightly oil 6 ramekin dishes and line the bases with discs of greased greaseproof paper. Pile the parfait mixture into the ramekins and smooth the tops with a palette knife. Freeze.
10. Make the sauce: mix all the ingredients in a small saucepan and bring to the boil. Reduce the heat and simmer for 10 minutes. Transfer to a bowl and chill in the refrigerator.
11. To serve: remove the parfaits from the freezer 10 minutes before serving. Run a knife around the inside edge of the ramekins and unmould each on to a chilled dessert plate. Peel away the paper from the top and spoon the sauce around. Serve immediately.

NOTE: Alternatively the parfait can be removed from the ramekins, put on to a plate and kept in the freezer until ready to be served.

Suggested dessert wine: AUSTRALIAN OR CALIFORNIAN ORANGE MUSCAT

Suggested main course: Beef or lamb

DRIED PEAR AND STAR ANISE ICE CREAM WITH CHOCOLATE FONDANT CAKE

A recent study, published by the American magazine *Bon Appétit*, showed that ice cream is eaten by three times more adults than children and also by more men than women. This is a very grown-up recipe, with a hint of *poire eau-de-vie* and a delicate taste of pear.

SERVES 6

110g/4oz no-need-to-soak dried pears
4 tablespoons poire eau-de-vie
250ml/8fl oz full-fat milk
340ml/12fl oz double cream
8 whole star anise
4 egg yolks
85g/3oz soft dark brown sugar

To serve
chocolate fondant cake (see page 135)

1. Chop the pears finely and mix with the *poire eau-de-vie* in a small bowl. Set aside.
2. Put the milk, cream and star anise into a large saucepan. Bring to the boil, then remove from the heat, cover and set aside to infuse for at least 30 minutes.
3. Beat the egg yolks and sugar with a wooden spoon until thoroughly mixed. Strain the milk and cream mixture on to the yolks and discard the star anise. Mix thoroughly and return to the pan. Cook over a low heat without boiling, stirring constantly, until the custard is thick enough to coat the back of the spoon.
4. Pour into a freezer-proof container and chill. Freeze the mixture for about 3 hours, until solid but still soft enough to give when pressed with a finger.
5. Tip the ice cream into a chilled bowl and break it up with a fork, then process or whisk until smooth, pale and creamy. Mix in the pears with the soaking liquid and mix well. Freeze again.
6. Transfer the ice cream to the refrigerator 20 minutes before serving. Serve with small slices of the chocolate fondant cake.

Suggested dessert wine: AUSTRALIAN LIQUEUR MUSCAT

Suggested main course: Lamb noisettes, duck breasts or a light fish dish

MASCARPONE ICE CREAM WITH GRILLED FIGS

Creamy and not too sweet, this ice cream is a perfect late summer/autumn dessert when figs are in season. It is also delicious with any fruit compote (see pages 116, 119 and 120).

SERVES 6

85g/3oz caster sugar
100ml/3fl oz water
1 vanilla pod, split in half lengthwise
5 egg yolks
560g/1¼lb Mascarpone cheese
55ml/2fl oz golden syrup
290ml/½ pint buttermilk

To serve
grilled figs (see page 122)

1. Put the sugar, water and vanilla pod into a saucepan and dissolve the sugar over a low heat, stirring.
2. In a large bowl, beat the egg yolks well. When the sugar has dissolved completely, bring the syrup up to boiling point and boil to the thread stage (see page 42). Allow to cool for 1 minute, then remove the vanilla pod, scrape out the black seeds and return them to the syrup.
3. Whisk the egg yolks and gradually pour in the sugar syrup, making sure it does not touch the beaters or it will solidify. Whisk until the mixture is very thick and will leave a ribbon trail. Leave to cool, whisking occasionally.
4. Whisk in the Mascarpone, golden syrup and buttermilk until thoroughly blended. Pass the mixture through a sieve into a freezer-proof container and freeze.
5. When the ice cream is half frozen, whisk again and return to the freezer. Transfer to the refrigerator 20 minutes before serving.
6. To serve: place 2 grilled figs on each dessert plate with a generous serving of ice cream.

Suggested dessert wine: SWEET OLOROSO SHERRY

Suggested main course: A light main course

NOUGAT ICE CREAM WITH RASPBERRY SAUCE

This recipe requires some advance preparation, but no ice-cream machine or food processor is needed.

SERVES 6

45g/1½oz caster sugar
100g/3½oz clear honey
4 tablespoons water
3 egg whites
150ml/¼ pint double cream
140g/5oz praline (see page 187)
110g/4oz mixed glacé fruit (cherries, angelica, orange and lemon peel), finely chopped

To decorate
4 sprigs of fresh mint

To serve
raspberry sauce (see page 210)

1. Wet and line a 450g/1lb loaf tin with clingfilm.
2. In a medium saucepan, combine the sugar, honey and water. Cook over a low heat without stirring until the sugar has completely dissolved. Increase the heat and cook to the thread stage (see page 42).
3. Meanwhile, whisk the egg whites to stiff peaks. Pour the sugar syrup steadily on to the egg whites, whisking all the time, but taking care that the syrup does not strike the beaters where it would cool and harden. Continue whisking until all the sugar has been absorbed and the meringue is completely cold.
4. Lightly whip the cream and gently fold it into the meringue together with the praline crumbs and glacé fruit.
5. Pour the mixture into the prepared loaf tin and freeze.
6. To serve: turn the ice cream on to a chopping board and cut into 4 slices. Place a slice on each individual serving plate and drizzle with the raspberry sauce. Decorate with a mint sprig and serve immediately.

Suggested dessert wine: MOSCATO D'ASTI/MUSCAT DE BEAUMES-DE-VENISE

Suggested main course: A 'Provencale' main course.

ICED ZABAGLIONE WITH PRUNES

A classic Italian dessert whose name derives from *sapillare* in the Neapolitan dialect, meaning 'to foam'. It is traditionally served tepid (making the name of this dessert something of a culinary licence) and it can be flavoured with any sweet wine or spirit or even with non-alcoholic flavours, like vanilla, lemon or coffee.

SERVES 6

140g/5oz prunes, stoned and roughly chopped
150ml/¼ pint strong hot freshly brewed Earl Grey tea
4 egg yolks
110g/4oz caster sugar
4 tablespoons Marsala
290ml/½ pint double cream
½ teaspoon ground cinnamon

To decorate
cocoa powder

To serve
tuiles amandines (see page 233)

1. Put the prunes into a bowl and cover with the tea. Leave to soak for 15 minutes. Drain and discard the tea.
2. Place the egg yolks and sugar in a large heatproof bowl and fit it over (not in) a saucepan of simmering water. Whisk until the mixture is light, thick and fluffy.
3. Remove the bowl from the heat and continue whisking until slightly cooled. Add the Marsala and chill for 10 minutes.
4. Whip the cream to soft peaks and, using a large metal spoon, mix gently into the chilled zabaglione. Mix in the prunes and the cinnamon.
5. Spoon the mixture into individual serving glasses or a glass bowl and freeze overnight until firm.
6. Transfer the zabaglione to the refrigerator 30 minutes before serving. Dust lightly with sifted cocoa powder just before serving.
7. Serve with tuiles amandines.

Suggested dessert wine: MARSALA/ RICH MADEIRA

Suggested main course: Poultry or fish

FROZEN RASPBERRY YOGHURT

Quick, simple and delicious, this recipe can also be made using strawberries.

SERVES 6

450g/1lb raspberries
110g/4oz icing sugar
425ml/¾ pint Greek yoghurt
2 egg whites
3 tablespoons caster sugar

To serve
chocolate sauce *(see page 213)*

1. Process half the raspberries and pass through a sieve to make a purée. In a large bowl, mix the raspberry purée with the icing sugar and yoghurt until thoroughly blended. Cover and chill in the refrigerator for 30 minutes.
2. In a medium bowl, whisk the egg whites to medium peaks. Add the caster sugar and continue whisking until shiny and stiff.
3. Gently fold the raspberry yoghurt mixture into the meringue until well combined. Pour into a freezer-proof container and freeze the mixture for about 3 hours, until solid but still soft enough to give when pressed with a finger.
4. Tip the ice cream into a chilled bowl and break it up with a fork, then process or whisk until smooth and pale. Gently mix in the remaining raspberries and freeze again.
5. Transfer the frozen yoghurt to the refrigerator 20 minutes before serving. Serve with warm chocolate sauce.

NOTE: Ice creams made with yoghurt inevitably have a crystal-like texture. The more they are whisked, the smoother they become. If you have an ice-cream machine, however, they will be almost as smooth as other ice creams.

Suggested dessert wine: AUSTRALIAN LIQUEUR MUSCAT

Suggested main course: Seafood

TROPICAL FRUIT AND FROZEN YOGHURT CUP WITH PINEAPPLE SAUCE

It is important to choose a ripe pineapple since they don't ripen further after they have been picked. Ripe pineapples have a strong aroma and the leaves from the top pull out easily. This refreshing dessert does not take long to prepare and most of the preparation can be done in advance.

SERVES 6

For the fruit salad
1 mango, peeled, stoned and diced
1 papaya, halved, seeded, peeled and diced
1 banana, peeled and diced
½ fresh pineapple, peeled, cored and diced
juice of ½ lime
2 teaspoons icing sugar

For the sauce
85g/3oz caster sugar
110g/4oz soft dark brown sugar
150ml/¼ pint water
150ml/¼ pint unsweetened pineapple juice
30g/1oz unsalted butter
2 tablespoons dark rum (optional)

To serve
1.14 litres/2 pint quantity honey yoghurt ice-cream, softened (see page 197)

1. Make the fruit salad: mix all the ingredients in a bowl and chill in the refrigerator while making the sauce.
2. Make the sauce: combine the sugars, water, juice and butter in a heavy saucepan. Cook over a low heat until the sugar has dissolved completely. Bring to the boil, turn down the heat and simmer for about 10 minutes, or until the sauce is slightly reduced and thickened. Remove from the heat and mix in the rum. Allow to cool slightly.
3. To serve: in 6 large tall glasses, start layering first with the fruit salad, then spoonfuls of frozen yoghurt and a drizzle of the sauce. Finish layering with the fruit salad and drizzle generously with the remaining sauce. Serve immediately.

NOTES: The fruit salad can be prepared up to 6 hours in advance without the bananas. Add them just before assembling the dessert.

The sauce can be made up to 2 days in advance and reheated just before assembling the dessert.

Just one type of fruit, e.g. 1 whole ripe pineapple, or 3 large mangoes, may be used.

Suggested dessert wine: MUSCAT DE BEAUMES-DE-VENISE

Suggested main course: Roast meat or a rich pasta dish

ROASTED PEARS WITH BLACK PEPPER AND HONEY YOGHURT ICE CREAM

This recipe is very easy to make and tastes delicious. The unusual combination of black pepper and honey is a very successful one.

SERVES 4

4 pears
45g/1½oz unsalted butter
55g/2oz caster sugar
freshly ground black pepper
3 tablespoons clear honey
2 tablespoons lemon juice

To serve
honey yoghurt ice cream (see page 197)

To decorate
fresh mint leaves

1. Preheat the oven to 200°C/400°F/gas mark 6.
2. Wash the pears and cut in half lengthwise. Scoop out the cores with a melon scooper and leave the stems intact.
3. Melt the butter in a sauté pan until hot. Add the pears, cut sides down, and cook for 4–5 minutes, or until lightly browned. Gently transfer the pears to a gratin dish, browned sides up. Sprinkle with the sugar and season with pepper.
4. Bake the pears for 20 minutes, or until tender. Remove from the oven and allow to cool slightly.
5. Mix the honey with the lemon juice.
6. To serve: place 2 pear halves on each dessert plate and spoon some honey yoghurt ice cream on the side. Drizzle the pears and ice cream with the honey and lemon mixture. Decorate with a mint leaf and serve immediately.

NOTE: The pears can be prepared up to the end of stage 3 up to 6 hours in advance and kept in the refrigerator.
Just before serving, reheat the pears in a moderate oven (180°C/350°F/gas mark 4) for about 10 minutes.

Suggested dessert wine: MUSCAT DE BEAUMES-DE-VENISE/MOSCATEL DE VALENCIA

Suggested main course: A game or vegetarian dish

HONEY YOGHURT ICE CREAM

This delicious recipe has been used with kind permission of the authors of *Leith's Contemporary Cooking.*

SERVES 4

4 egg yolks
4 tablespoons clear honey
290ml/½ pint milk
500g/18oz Greek yoghurt

1. Put the egg yolks and honey into a bowl and whisk with electric beaters until pale, thick and creamy.
2. Warm the milk in a saucepan, then pour on to the yolk and honey mixture, stirring steadily.
3. Return the milk to the saucepan. Stir over a low heat for about 5 minutes, until the mixture is thick enough to coat the back of the spoon. Do not boil.
4. Pour into a large bowl and beat in the yoghurt using a wooden spoon.
5. Pour into a freezer-proof container, cover with a lid, and leave to become cold. Freeze for 2–3 hours, or until solid.
6. Remove from the freezer and allow to soften at room temperature. Place in a food processor and whizz to remove the ice crystals. Return the mixture to the container, cover and return to the freezer for at least 2 hours.
7. Transfer the ice cream to the refrigerator 20 minutes before serving.

NOTE: Ice creams made with yoghurt inevitably have a crystle-like texture. The more they are whisked, the smoother they become. If you have an ice-cream machine, however, they will be almost as smooth as other ice creams.

Suggested dessert wine: BUAL/ MALMSEY MADEIRA

Suggested main course: Vegetarian or pasta

LEMON SORBET

Refreshing and tangy, fruit sorbets make palate-cleansing desserts on their own, in a combination of flavours, or together with ice cream.

SERVES 4

thinly pared zest and juice of 3 lemons
140g/5oz granulated sugar
570ml/1 pint water
½ egg white

1. Place the lemon zest, sugar and water in a heavy saucepan. Dissolve the sugar over a low heat and, when completely dissolved, boil rapidly to the short thread stage (see page 42).
2. Remove from the heat and allow to cool completely. When the syrup is cold, add the lemon juice and strain.
3. Freeze for 30 minutes, or until beginning to solidify.
4. Whisk the egg white until stiff and fold into the mixture.
5. Return to the freezer until firm.

NOTE: If you have a food processor, allow the lemon syrup to freeze and then whizz until soft. Pour in the egg white, through the funnel, whizzing all the time. Freeze until firm.

Suggested dessert wine: MOSCATO D'ASTI

Suggested main course: Any rich dish

STRAWBERRY SORBET

SERVES 4

170g/6oz caster sugar
570ml/1 pint water
juice of ½ lemon or small orange
340g/12oz fresh or frozen strawberries
1 egg white

1. Place the sugar and water in a heavy saucepan. Dissolve the sugar over a low heat. When completely dissolved, boil gently for 5 minutes. Add the lemon or orange juice and cool.
2. Liquidize or mash the strawberries to a pulp and add the syrup. Place in a bowl in the freezer for 30 minutes or until beginning to solidify.
3. Whisk the egg whites until stiff and fold into the mixture.
4. Return to the freezer until firm.

NOTE: If you have a food processor, allow the strawberry syrup to freeze, then whizz until soft. Pour in the egg white, through the funnel, whizzing all the time. Freeze until firm.

Suggested dessert wine: MOSCATO D'ASTI

Suggested main course: Any rich dish

PASSIONFRUIT SORBET

SERVES 6

140g/5oz granulated sugar
425ml/¾ pint water
thinly pared zest and juice of 1 lemon
450g/1lb passionfruit pulp (from about 32 passionfruits)
½ egg white

1. Dissolve the sugar in the water in a heavy saucepan. When completely dissolved, add the lemon zest and boil rapidly for 5 minutes, or until the syrup is tacky.
2. Sieve the passionfruit pulp and add to the syrup with the lemon juice. Cool.
3. Place in a bowl in the freezer until half-frozen.
4. Tip into a chilled bowl and whisk well. Refreeze until almost solid.
5. Whisk the egg white until very stiff.
6. Tip the sorbet into another chilled bowl and break up. Whisk until smooth and fold in the egg white.
7. Freeze again until firm.
8. If the ice is not absolutely creamy and smooth, give it one more freezing and whisking.

NOTE: If you have a food processor, allow the passionfruit, syrup and lemon juice to freeze. Defrost slightly, then whizz until soft. Pour the egg white in, through the funnel, whizzing all the time. Freeze until firm.

Suggested dessert wine: MOSCATO D'ASTI

Suggested main course: Any rich dish

APPLE SORBET

SERVES 4

4 Cox's apples
160g/5½oz caster sugar
2 tablespoons Calvados
juice of 1 lemon
1 egg white

1. Peel, core and quarter the apples.
2. Put the apples into a saucepan with the sugar and enough water to just cover them. Poach gently for 20 minutes or until glassy.
3. Remove the apples and reduce the cooking liquor, by boiling rapidly to the short thread stage (see page 42). Purée the apples, syrup, Calvados and lemon juice together in a food processor or blender.
4. Allow to cool, then pour into a freezer container and freeze.
5. When nearly frozen, place the sorbet in a processor and whizz briefly. Gradually add the unwhisked egg white with the motor running. The mixture will fluff up tremendously. Return to the container and freeze until firm.

Suggested dessert wine: MOSCATO D'ASTI

Suggested main course: Any rich dish

PEAR SORBET

SERVES 4

4 ripe William pears
160g/5½oz caster or icing sugar
juice of 2 lemons
1 egg white, lightly whisked

1. Peel, core and quarter the pears.
2. Put the pears into a saucepan with the sugar and enough water to just cover them. Poach gently for 20 minutes or until glassy.
3. Remove the pears and reduce the cooking liquor by boiling rapidly to the short thread stage (see page 42). Purée the pears, syrup and lemon juice together in a food processor or blender.
4. Allow to cool, then pour into a freezer container and freeze.
5. When nearly frozen, fold in the egg white and freeze until firm.

NOTE: If you have a food processor, allow the sorbet to freeze and then defrost until half-frozen. Whizz in the food processor and gradually add the egg white, unwhisked. It will fluff up tremendously. Return to the container and freeze until firm.

Suggested dessert wine: MOSCATO D'ASTI

Suggested main course: Any rich dish

FROZEN CHOCOLATE TRUFFLES

These are decadence itself. Rich, delicious and a real treat.

MAKES ABOUT 30

180ml/6fl oz double cream
110g/4oz caster sugar
3 egg yolks
225g/8oz dark, very good-quality chocolate, chopped
2 tablespoons Amaretto or other nut liqueur (optional)
85g/3oz cocoa powder

To serve
pear sorbet (see page 202)

1. Bring the cream slowly to the boil in a medium heavy saucepan.
2. Mix the sugar and egg yolks in a bowl. Pour the hot cream on to the mixture, stirring constantly. Mix well and return to the pan.
3. Stir over a low heat without boiling, until the custard is thick enough to coat the back of the spoon. Remove the pan from the heat, add the chopped chocolate and mix thoroughly. Mix in the liqueur, if using.
4. Transfer the mixture to a freezer-proof container and freeze for about 3 hours or up to 24, until firm enough to shape.
5. To shape: sift the cocoa powder on to a large plate. Take 1 rounded teaspoon of the truffle mixture and shape roughly into a round. Roll in the cocoa powder and arrange in a single layer in a container lined with greaseproof paper.
6. Freeze for up to 1 month. Serve the truffles frozen: they will keep a soft consistency, but will be delightfully cold.

Suggested dessert wine: AUSTRALIAN LIQUEUR MUSCAT/YOUNG LBV PORT

Suggested main course: Any main course

SAUCES AND CRÈMES

FRESH APRICOT SAUCE

During the summer, when apricots are widely available, this sauce can be made in larger quantities and kept in airtight containers in the freezer or sterilized jars.

450g/1lb fresh apricots
140g/5oz icing sugar
3 tablespoons water
juice of 1 lemon

1. Halve the apricots and reserve the stones. Place the apricots and stones in a saucepan with the icing sugar and water. Cook over a low heat, covered, until the apricots are very soft. Remove from the heat and allow to cool slightly. Remove the stones and discard.
2. Mix the apricots, any juice from cooking and the lemon juice in a food processor or blender. Blend to a fine purée (if too thick add a little more water).
3. Pass the purée through a fine sieve (chinois) and add more icing sugar if not sweet enough. Chill in the refrigerator for at least 3 hours before serving.

NOTE: This sauce can be made up to 3 days in advance and kept in the refrigerator. Depending on how ripe the apricots are, adjust the sweetness at the end if required.

APRICOT GLAZE

3 tablespoons apricot jam
2 tablespoons water
juice of ½ lemon

1. Place all the ingredients in a heavy saucepan.
2. Bring slowly to the boil, stirring gently (avoid beating in bubbles) until syrupy in consistency. Strain.

NOTE: Use when still warm, as the glaze becomes too stiff to manage when cold. It will keep warm in a heatproof bowl set over a saucepan of very hot water.

PEAR SAUCE

This delicate sauce is a delicious accompaniment to rich chocolate cakes (see pages 135, 139), making a good alternative to cream.

500g/1lb 2oz pears
100ml/3fl oz water
85g/3oz icing sugar
juice of 1 lemon
1 tablespoon poire eau-de-vie (optional)

1. Peel and core the pears and chop into small pieces.
2. In a medium saucepan, mix the pears, water and icing sugar. Cook over a low heat until the pears have become a purée.
3. Transfer the pears and cooking liquid to a blender or food processor, add the lemon juice and process to a smooth purée. If too thick, add a few tablespoons of water. Pass through a fine sieve (chinois) and add more lemon juice if too sweet, more sifted icing sugar if not sweet enough.
4. Transfer the sauce to a bowl and add the *poire eau-de-vie*, if using. Serve cold.

RASPBERRY SAUCE

This very versatile sauce can be made using fresh or frozen raspberries with equally good results. It gives a nice touch to a simple dessert and is particularly good with meringues. It can be made a day ahead and kept covered in the refrigerator.

370g/13oz raspberries
140g/5oz icing sugar
juice of 1 lemon

1. In a food processor, blend the raspberries, icing sugar and lemon juice together for a few seconds.
2. Push through a fine nylon sieve (chinois) and add more sugar if not sweet enough, more lemon juice if too sweet.
3. Chill in the refrigerator for at least 3 hours. Serve cold.

VARIATION
Strawberry sauce: Same method as above, using 450g/1lb cleaned and hulled strawberries.

RASPBERRY COULIS

This coulis has a shinier appearance than the raspberry sauce on page 210.

340g/12oz raspberries
juice of ½ lemon
70ml/2½fl oz sugar syrup (see page 42)

1. Whizz all the ingredients together in a food processor or blender, and push through a conical strainer.
2. If too thin, the coulis can be thickened by boiling rapidly in a heavy saucepan. Stir well to prevent it from catching.

BOYSENBERRY SAUCE

Use blackberries if boysenberries are not available.

1 vanilla pod, split in half lengthwise
450g/1lb boysenberries
100ml/3fl oz crème de Cassis
30g/1oz caster sugar

1. Scrape the seeds from the vanilla pod into a heavy medium saucepan. Add the pod, boysenberries, crème de Cassis and sugar. Mix well and cook over a medium heat for about 15 minutes, stirring occasionally, until the berries thaw and the sugar dissolves.
2. Bring the mixture to the boil, then remove from the heat. Discard the vanilla pod and purée the mixture in a food processor or blender. Sieve into a bowl. Cover and chill in the refrigerator until required.

NOTES: The sauce can be made up to a day in advance and kept covered in the refrigerator.

To serve as a compote with Greek yoghurt, mix 225g/8oz berries into the finished sauce.

CHOCOLATE SAUCE

This is a good-with-everything, easy-to-make chocolate sauce. It is essential to use top-quality dark chocolate to achieve a good result. It can be made up to a week in advance and stored in an airtight container in the refrigerator, then very gently reheated before use.

190ml/⅓ pint double cream
45g/1½oz caster sugar
1 teaspoon vanilla essence
140g/4oz dark good-quality chocolate, chopped

1. Combine the cream and sugar in a heavy medium saucepan. Stir over a medium heat until the sugar has dissolved completely. Bring to the boil, then remove from the heat.
2. Add the vanilla and chopped chocolate. Whisk until the chocolate has melted and the sauce is smooth and shiny.
3. Serve warm.

WHITE CHOCOLATE AND ORANGE SAUCE

This sauce can be made up to 3 days in advance and reheated gently before serving.

150ml/¼ pint single cream
grated zest and juice of ½ orange
225g/8oz white chocolate, chopped
1 teaspoon Cointreau (optional)

1. Combine the cream, orange zest and juice in a small saucepan. Bring to the boil, then remove from the heat.
2. Add the chopped chocolate off the heat and stir until the chocolate has melted completely and the sauce is smooth and shiny.
3. Stir in the Cointreau, if using. Serve warm or cold.

WHITE CHOCOLATE AND VANILLA CREAM

This recipe is a treat for white-chocolate lovers and very simple to make. It is delicious with fruit flans as an interesting alternative to pouring cream.

250ml/8fl oz double cream
1 vanilla pod, split in half lengthwise
200g/7oz good-quality white chocolate, chopped

1. In a small pan, bring half the cream and the vanilla pod to the boil, then remove from the heat. Scrape the seeds from the vanilla pod back into the cream and discard the pod.
2. Add the chopped chocolate and whisk gently until the chocolate has melted completely. Allow the mixture to cool to room temperature.
3. In a bowl, whisk the remaining cream to stiff peaks. Using a large metal spoon, gently fold in the chocolate cream mixture. Pour into a container and chill for about 1 hour, until firm. Remove from the refrigerator 20 minutes before serving.

NOTE: This recipe can be made up to 3 days in advance and kept in the refrigerator, then very gently reheated before use.

CAPPUCCINO SAUCE

It is essential to use a freshly brewed coffee for this sauce or it will taste insipid. It can be made up to 3 days in advance and reheated gently before serving.

150ml/¼ pint strong, freshly brewed coffee
150ml/¼ pint double cream
85g/3oz soft light brown sugar
½ teaspoon ground cinnamon
110g/4oz milk chocolate, finely chopped

1. In a medium saucepan, mix together the coffee, cream, sugar and cinnamon. Cook over a low heat until the sugar has dissolved completely. Increase the heat and boil for 5 minutes or until the liquid is reduced by one-third.
2. Remove the pan from the heat, add the chocolate and stir until the chocolate has melted completely and the sauce is smooth and shiny. Serve warm over ice cream or with chocolate cake.

WARM CARAMEL SAUCE

Rich and thick, this sauce is good with any dessert, from ice creams to cakes and yoghurt. It can be made up to 3 days in advance and reheated gently just before serving.

225g/8oz granulated sugar
6 tablespoons hot water
190ml/⅓ pint double cream

1. Place the sugar with the water in a heavy saucepan and allow it to melt slowly over a low heat without stirring. When the sugar has melted completely, boil rapidly until it becomes a rich brown caramel (it is important to get a dark caramel or the sauce will taste very sweet with very little flavour).
2. Remove the pan from the heat and carefully add the cream. Put the pan back on the heat and stir until all the caramel has melted and the sauce is well blended. Serve at room temperature.

ORANGE AND CARAMEL SAUCE

This sauce can be made up to 2 days in advance and kept covered in the refrigerator.

2 oranges
225g/8oz granulated sugar
110ml/4fl oz water
1 tablespoon Grand Marnier (optional)

1. Pare 2 × 5cm/2in long strips of the orange zest and cut into fine shreds (julienne). Squeeze the oranges and reserve the juice.
2. Make the caramel: place the sugar with the water in a heavy saucepan.
3. Dissolve the sugar slowly without stirring or allowing the water to boil. Once all the sugar has dissolved, turn up the heat and boil until it is a good caramel colour. Immediately tip in the orange juice (it will fizz dangerously, so stand back).
4. Add the orange zest shreds and stir until any lumps have dissolved, then remove from the heat and allow to cool. Add the Grand Marnier, if using.

NOTE: This sauce can be made up to 2 days in advance and kept covered in the refrigerator. For a richer version, add 3 tablespoons double cream to the finished sauce and mix thoroughly.

MAPLE AND VANILLA SAUCE

Maple syrup has a very delicate and distinct taste that marries well with apples, nuts and berries. This recipe is particularly good served with baked apples (see page 109) or over ice cream.

150ml/¼ pint double cream
1 vanilla pod, split in half lengthwise
250ml/8fl oz pure maple syrup

1. In a medium saucepan, mix together the cream, vanilla pod and maple syrup. Cook over a low heat for 5 minutes, stirring occasionally. Remove the vanilla pod, scrape the seeds back into the sauce and discard the pod.
2. Serve warm.

NOTE: This sauce can be made up to 3 days in advance and kept covered in the refrigerator until needed. Reheat over a low heat, stirring.

BUTTERSCOTCH SAUCE

A rich, sweet sauce that will keep for a week in an airtight container in the refrigerator. Heat gently before serving.

225g/8oz caster sugar
150ml/¼ pint water
250ml/8fl oz double cream
45g/1½oz unsalted butter

1. Put the sugar and water into a saucepan over a medium heat. Allow the sugar to dissolve before bringing to the boil. Cook to a golden-brown, then remove from the heat.
2. Immediately add the cream and return to the heat. Stir to dissolve any lumps. Add the butter and stir until thoroughly blended.

HOT FUDGE SAUCE

This is a rich, smooth and delicious chocolate sauce that goes well with any ice cream. It can be made up to a week in advance and kept covered in the refrigerator. Reheat over a low heat before using.

170g/6oz icing sugar
140g/4oz unsalted butter, cut into cubes
150ml/¼ pint single cream
225g/8oz good-quality semi-sweet chocolate, chopped
1 teaspoon vanilla essence

1. In a saucepan, combine the icing sugar, butter and cream. Stir over a medium heat for about 10 minutes, until the butter has melted and the sauce is completely smooth and hot.
2. Remove the pan from the heat, add the chocolate and stir until melted and smooth. Stir in the vanilla and serve warm.

RED WINE SYRUP SAUCE

A great sauce to make with any left-over red wine. It keeps for a week covered in the refrigerator and adds a nice touch to cakes, ice creams or any plum or prune dessert.

290ml/½ pint dry red wine
255g/9oz caster sugar
2 cinnamon sticks

1. Put the wine, sugar and cinnamon into a medium saucepan and simmer gently until the sugar has dissolved. Increase the heat and boil for about 5 minutes or until the syrup is reduced by one-third. Remove the cinnamon and discard.
2. Transfer the sauce to a bowl and allow to cool, then chill in the refrigerator.

CRÈME CHANTILLY

150ml/¼ pint double cream
1 teaspoon icing sugar
2 drops of vanilla essence

1. Put all the ingredients into a chilled bowl and whisk with a balloon whisk, steadily but not too fast, for about 2 minutes or until the cream has thickened and doubled in volume.
2. Whisk faster for 30–40 seconds until the mixture is very fluffy and will form soft peaks.

NOTE: Chilling the ingredients and the bowl gives a lighter, whiter result.

CRÈME PÂTISSIÈRE

290ml/½ pint milk
2 egg yolks
55g/2oz caster sugar
20g/¾oz plain flour
20g/¾oz cornflour
vanilla essence

1. Scald the milk by bringing it to just below boiling point in a saucepan.
2. Cream the egg yolks with the sugar and a little of the milk and when pale, mix in the flours. Pour on the milk and mix well.
3. Return the mixture to the pan and bring slowly to the boil, stirring continuously. (It will go alarmingly lumpy, but don't worry, keep stirring vigorously and it will become smooth.) Allow to cool slightly, then add the vanilla.

CRÈME ANGLAISE (ENGLISH EGG CUSTARD)

290ml/½ pint milk
1 vanilla pod or a few drops of vanilla essence
2 egg yolks
1 tablespoon caster sugar

1. Heat the milk and vanilla pod, if using, and bring slowly to the boil.
2. Beat the egg yolks in a bowl with the sugar. Remove the vanilla pod, and pour the milk on to the yolks, stirring steadily. Mix well and return to the pan.
3. Stir over a low heat for about 5 minutes, until the mixture thickens sufficiently to coat the back of a spoon. Strain into a chilled bowl.
4. Add the vanilla essence, if using.

PASSIONFRUIT CRÈME ANGLAISE

570ml/1 pint milk
grated zest of ½ orange
4 passionfruit
85g/3oz sugar
6 egg yolks

1. Heat the milk with the orange zest and bring slowly to the boil.
2. Cut the passionfruit in half and scoop out the seeds and juice into a small bowl. Reserve.
3. In another bowl, whisk the sugar and egg yolks together until pale. Pour the hot milk on to the yolks, stirring steadily.
4. Return the milk to the pan and cook over a low heat for about 5 minutes, stirring well until the custard is thick enough to coat the back of the spoon.
5. Allow to cool slightly, then add the passionfruit pulp and seeds and mix thoroughly. Strain into a clean bowl, discarding the passionfruit seeds. Allow to cool, then chill well before using.

FRANGIPANE

A great dessert invention by the Italian pastry chefs of Catherine de Médicis in sixteenth-century France. She became the wife of King Henry II of France. Her enormous appetite, and the fifty Italian chefs she brought with her to the French court, helped to transform French cooking.

100g/3½oz butter
100g/3½oz caster sugar
1 egg, beaten
1 egg yolk
2 tablespoons Calvados or Kirsch
100g/3½oz ground almonds
100g/3½oz plain flour

1. Cream the butter in a bowl, gradually beat in the sugar and continue beating until the mixture is light and fluffy. Gradually add the whole egg and the yolk, beating well after each addition. Add the Calvados or Kirsch, then stir in the ground almonds and the flour.
2. Use as required.

NOTE: The frangipane can be made up to 3 days in advance and kept covered in the refrigerator. Let the mixture come to room temperature before using.

BISCUITS

PINE NUT SABLÉS

Literally meaning 'covered in sand', these dry, crumbly biscuits make a delicious accompaniment to sorbets and ice creams.

MAKES ABOUT 30

oil for greasing
85g/3oz pine nuts
55g/2oz unsalted butter
30g/1oz vegetable shortening
30g/1oz icing sugar, sifted
30g/1oz caster sugar, plus a little extra for sprinkling
125g/4½oz plain flour
½ teaspoon baking powder
a pinch of salt

1. Preheat the oven to 170°C/325°F/gas mark 3. Lightly oil a baking sheet.
2. Spread the pine nuts on an unoiled baking sheet and place in the oven for 8–10 minutes or until the nuts are lightly browned. Remove from the oven and transfer the nuts to a plate to cool (pine nuts burn very easily, so check after 5 minutes).
3. Reserve a few nuts for decorating the sablés and chop the remainder finely.
4. Cream the butter and shortening in a bowl until soft. Add the sugars and beat until well combined.
5. Sift the flour, baking powder and salt together twice. Add to the butter mixture together with the chopped nuts and mix thoroughly to form a soft dough.
6. Roll out teaspoonfuls of the mixture into balls and place on the prepared baking sheet. Press them lightly with the palm of the hand to form rounds about 1cm/½in high. Press a few whole pine nuts on top of each sablé and sprinkle lightly with caster sugar. Bake in the centre of the oven for about 30 minutes, or until they are light golden in colour. Transfer to a wire rack and leave to cool.

NOTE: These sablés can be made up to a week in advance and once cold kept in an airtight container in single layers between sheets of greaseproof paper.

ALMOND BISCUITS

MAKES 10–15

170g/6oz plain flour
100g/3½oz caster sugar
¼ teaspoon baking powder
¼ teaspoon salt
110g/4oz butter, cut into pieces
1 egg, lightly beaten
1 teaspoon almond essence
15–20 whole blanched almonds

1. Preheat the oven to 170°C/325°F/gas mark 3.
2. In a large bowl, sift together the flour, sugar, baking powder and salt. Rub in the butter with the fingertips until the mixture resembles coarse breadcrumbs.
3. Add the egg and almond essence and mix to a soft dough, first with a knife, then with one hand.
4. Roll the mixture into 2.5cm/1in balls with the fingers and place well apart on two ungreased baking sheets. Press an almond into the centre of each biscuit, lightly flattening the top. Chill in the refrigerator for 15 minutes.
5. Bake in the centre of the oven for 10–15 minutes, or until the biscuits are just beginning to brown underneath.
6. While the biscuits are hot, ease them off the baking sheets with a palette knife or fish slice and cool on a wire rack. Once stone-cold and crisp, store in an airtight container.

TUILES AMANDINES

MAKES 25

oil for greasing
30g/1oz blanched almonds
2 egg whites
110g/4oz caster sugar
55g/2oz plain flour
½ teaspoon vanilla essence
55g/2oz butter, melted and cooled

1. Preheat the oven to 180°C/350°F/gas mark 4. Lightly oil at least three baking sheets and a rolling pin or line the baking sheets with silicone baking paper.
2. Cut the almonds into fine slivers or shreds.
3. Place the egg whites in a bowl. Beat in the sugar with a fork. The egg white should be frothy but by no means snowy. Sift in the flour and add the vanilla essence and almonds. Mix with the fork.
4. Add the melted butter to the mixture. Stir well.
5. Place teaspoonfuls of the mixture at least 13cm/5in apart on the prepared baking sheets and flatten well.
6. Bake in the centre of the oven for about 6 minutes until pale biscuit-coloured in the middle and a good brown at the edges. Remove from the oven and cool for a few seconds.
7. Lift the biscuits off carefully with a palette knife. Lay them, while still warm and pliable, over the rolling pin to form them into a slightly curved shape. Leave on a wire rack to cool completely.
8. When cold, store in an airtight tin.

MACAROONS

Macaroons are particularly good made with freshly ground blanched almonds.

MAKES 25

110g/4oz ground almonds
170g/6oz caster sugar
1 teaspoon plain flour
2 egg whites
2 drops of vanilla essence
rice paper for baking

To decorate
split blanched almonds

1. Preheat the oven to 180°C/350°F/gas mark 4.
2. Mix together the ground almonds, sugar and flour.
3. Add the egg whites and vanilla essence. Beat very well. Leave to stand for 5 minutes. Beat again for 1 minute.
4. Line a baking sheet with rice paper or silicone baking paper and with a teaspoon put on small heaps of the mixture, well apart.
5. Place a split almond on each macaroon and bake in the oven for 20 minutes. Leave on a wire rack to cool completely.

NOTES: To use this recipe for petits fours the mixture must be put out in very tiny blobs on the rice paper. Two macaroons can then be sandwiched together with a little stiff apricot jam and served in petits fours paper cases.

Ratafia biscuits are tiny macaroons with almond essence added.

HAZELNUT AND COFFEE BISCUITS

MAKES ABOUT 32

oil for greasing
110g/4oz unsalted butter, softened
30g/1oz icing sugar
1½ teaspoons coffee essence
85g/3oz plain flour
30g/1oz cornflour
30g/1oz whole hazelnuts, skinned

1. Lightly oil two baking sheets.
2. Cream the butter in a bowl until soft. Beat in the sugar until light and fluffy. Add the coffee essence.
3. Sift together the flour and cornflour and work into the butter mixture, then beat until very soft and smooth.
4. Spoon the mixture into a forcing bag fitted with a 1cm/½in star nozzle. Squeeze gently to get rid of any pockets of air. Hold the bag upright in your right hand and, using your left hand to guide the nozzle, pipe 2.5cm/1in star shapes, allowing some room between them to spread. Place a hazelnut on top of each. Chill the trays in the refrigerator for 1 hour.
5. Preheat the oven to 180°C/350°F/gas mark 4.
6. Bake the biscuits in the centre of the oven for about 10–12 minutes, or until lightly browned.
7. Transfer the biscuits to a wire rack and allow to cool completely before storing in an airtight container where they will keep for up to a week.

NOTE: The biscuits can be prepared up to the end of stage 4, then frozen and allowed to defrost before baking.

TRIPLE CHOCOLATE AND CINNAMON BISCUITS

These rich, luscious, small bite-sized chocolate biscuits can be served with ice creams and sorbets.

MAKES ABOUT 25

oil for greasing
30g/1oz plain flour
30g/1oz cocoa powder
1½ teaspoons ground cinnamon
¼ teaspoon baking powder
a pinch of salt
85g/3oz unsalted butter, softened
100g/3½oz caster sugar
3 eggs, beaten
225g/8oz bitter dark chocolate, melted and cooled
140g/5oz walnuts, roughly chopped
170g/6oz milk chocolate, finely chopped

1. Preheat the oven to 180°C/350°F/gas mark 4. Lightly oil one or two baking sheets.
2. Sift together the flour, cocoa, cinnamon, baking powder and salt.
3. Beat the butter in a large bowl, add the sugar and beat until light and creamy. Add the eggs gradually, beating well after each addition. Stir in the melted chocolate and mix well. Add the sifted flour and cocoa mixture and mix thoroughly. Finally, stir in the nuts and chopped chocolate.
4. Drop teaspoons of the mixture on to the prepared baking sheets. Bake in the centre of the oven for about 8–10 minutes, or until the biscuits look dry and cracked but feel soft when lightly pressed. Using a spatula or fish slice, transfer the biscuits to a wire rack and leave to cool completely.

NOTE: When completely cold, the biscuits can be stored in an airtight container between layers of greaseproof paper for up to a week.

GLOSSARY

Bain-marie: A baking tin or roasting pan half-filled with hot water in which terrines, custards, etc. stand while cooking. The food is protected from direct fierce heat and cooks in a gentle, steamy atmosphere.
Bake blind: To bake a flan case while empty. In order to prevent the sides falling in or the base bubbling up, the pastry is usually lined with paper and filled with 'blind beans' (see below). For instructions on baking a pastry case blind, see page 100.
Bavarois: Creamy pudding made with eggs and cream and set with gelatine.
Blind beans: Dried beans, peas, rice or pasta used to fill pastry cases temporarily during baking.
Caramel: Sugar cooked to a toffee. See stages in sugar syrup concentration chart, see page 42.
Clarified butter: Butter that has been separated from milk particles and other impurities which cause it to look cloudy when melted, and to burn easily when heated. For instructions on clarifying butter, see page 25.
Cream, to: To beat ingredients such as butter and fat together, when making a sponge cake, for example.
Crêpes: Thin pancakes. For recipe, see page 106.
Dropping consistency: The consistency where a mixture will drop reluctantly from a spoon, neither pouring off nor obstinately adhering.
Egg wash: Beaten raw egg, sometimes with salt added, used for glazing pastry to give it a shine when baked.
Fold: To mix with a gentle lifting motion, rather than to stir vigorously. The aim is to avoid beating out air while mixing.
Glaze: To cover with a thin layer of melted jam (for fruit flans) or syrup (for rum baba), butter or oil.
Gratiner, gratin: To brown under a grill after the surface of the dish has been sprinkled with breadcrumbs and butter or sugar. Dishes finished like this are sometimes called gratiné or au gratin.
Moule-à-manqué: French cake tin with sloping sides. The resulting cake has a wider base than top, and is about 2.5cm/1in high.
Panade or panada: Very thick mixture used as a base for soufflés, etc., usually made from milk, butter and flour.
Pass: To strain or push through a sieve.
Pâtisserie: Sweet cakes and pastries. Also, a cake shop.
Praline: Almonds cooked in sugar until the mixture caramelizes, then cooled and crushed to a powder. Used for flavouring desserts and ice cream. For recipe, see page 187.
Purée: Liquidized, sieved or finely mashed fruit or vegetables.

Reduce: To reduce the amount of liquid by rapid boiling, causing evaporation and consequent strengthening of flavour in the remaining liquid.

Relax or rest: Of pastry: to set aside in a cool place to allow the gluten (which will have expanded during rolling) to contract. This lessens the danger of shrinking in the oven. Of batters: to set aside to allow the starch cells to swell, giving a lighter result when cooked.

Sauter: Method of frying in a deep-frying pan or *sautoir*. The food is continually tossed or shaken so that it browns quickly and evenly.

Scald: Of milk: to heat until on the point of boiling, when some movement can be seen at the edges of the pan but there is no overall bubbling.

Soft ball: The term used to describe sugar syrup reduced by boiling to sufficient thickness to form soft balls when dropped into cold water and rubbed between finger and thumb. See stages in sugar syrup concentration chart, page 42.

Tammy: A fine muslin cloth through which sauces are sometimes forced. After this treatment they look beautifully smooth and shiny. Tammy cloths have recently been replaced by blenders or liquidizers, which give much the same effect.

Tammy strainer: A fine mesh strainer, conical in shape, used to produce the effect described under Tammy, above.

To the thread: Of sugar boiling. Term used to denote degree of thickness achieved when reducing syrup, i.e. the syrup will form threads if tested between a wet finger and thumb. Short thread: about 1cm/1in; long thread: 2cm/2in or more. See stages in sugar syrup concentration chart, page 42.

Well: A hollow or dip made in a pile or bowlful of flour, exposing the worktop or the bottom of the bowl, into which other ingredients are placed prior to mixing.

Zest: The thin skin of an orange or lemon, used to give flavour. Zest should be very thinly pared without any of the bitter white pith.

BIBLIOGRAPHY

BOOKS IN ENGLISH

Brillat-Savarin, Jean Anthelm: *The Physiology of Taste, or Meditation on Transcendental Gastronomy*, translated and annotated by M.F.K. Fisher (North Point Press: San Francisco, 1986)

Dowell, Philip and Bailey, Adrian, *The Book of Ingredients* (Mermaid Books: London, 1980)

Hobhouse, Henry, *Seeds of Change – Five Plants That Transformed Mankind* (Papermac: London, 1992)

MacClancy, Jeremy, *Consuming Culture* (Chapmans: London, 1992)

Ortiz, Elisabeth Lambert, *The Encyclopedia of Herbs, Spices and Flavourings* (Dorling Kindersley: London, 1992)

Quillin, Patrick, *Healing Nutrients* (Penguin Books: London, 1987)

Rinzler, Carol Ann, *Food Facts and What They Really Mean* (Bloomsbury: London, 1988)

Tannahill, Reay, *Food in History* (Penguin Books: London, 1988)

Visser, Margaret, *Much Depends on Dinner: the extraordinary history and mythology, allure and obsession, perils and taboos, of an ordinary meal* (Penguin Books: London, 1986)

BOOKS IN FRENCH

Apfeldorfer, Gérard, *Je mange, donc je suis: surpoids et troubles du comportement alimentaire* (Editions Payot & Rivages: Paris, 1993)

Charrette, Jacques and Vence, Céline, *Le grand livre de la pâtisserie et des desserts* (Edition Albin Michel SA: Paris, 1995)

Dumas, Alexandre, *Le grand dictionnaire de cuisine* (Édit-France: Paris, 1995)

La gourmandise, delices d'un péché, Série Mutations/Mangeur numéra 140 (Editions Autrement: Paris, 1993)

Le mangeur, menus, mots et maux, Série Mutations/Mangeur numéra 138 (Editions Autrement: Paris, 1993)

INDEX

Pagination in **bold** denotes the main reference among several page references